How to Find the Right Pastor

A HANDBOOK FOR PASTORAL AND STAFF SEARCH COMMITTEES

RON HUNTER JR.
DAVID C. GIBBS III

randall house

RandallHouse.com

ISBN: 9781614841623

What Others Are Saying

This book will save pulpit committees countless hours of unproductive "wheel spinning." It should be the first investment in the pursuit of a new pastor.

Dr. Mark L. Bailey
Chancellor and Sr. Professor of Bible Exposition, Dallas Theological Seminary

I have worked with many local churches over the years as they have searched for a new pastor. If I had had this book, I would have put it in their hands as a great tool in helping them search for their next pastor. Gibbs and Hunter have given the committee and individuals a tremendous guide to find the right pastor for their church. The most important feature about this book is that it covers all the necessary issues and questions and qualification needed for this very important position in the local church.

Dr. Elmer L. Towns
Co-Founder, Liberty University, Lynchburg, Virginia

How to find the right pastor for your congregation is one of the most important processes a church can undertake. While finding the right leader can be difficult, I hope you take advantage of this great tool to ease the burden and guide your church to the right leader at the right time.

J. Kevin Ingram
President, Manhattan Christian College, Manhattan, Kansas

A bad hire at any level, much less the senior pastor, is devastating to a church family. Churches will inevitably find themselves formulating and leading search committees. Unfortunately, most are ill-equipped to conduct the monumental task of finding the man of God who will lead their congregation. Ron Hunter and David Gibbs offer a much-needed road map that takes the guesswork out of the process. Every church should have this resource on hand.

Robby Gallaty, Ph.D.
Pastor, Long Hollow Church
Author of *Replicate* and *The Forgotten Jesus*

***How to Find the Right Pastor* is a marvelous, well-organized, and thoughtfully designed handbook for selecting pastoral leadership and church staff members in various size congregations and in diverse denominational settings. Highly recommended!**

David S. Dockery, Ph.D.
President, Southwestern Baptist Theological Seminary

David Gibbs and Ron Hunter have prepared a masterclass for churches to use as they consider how to find their next pastor.

Rev. Jay Therell
President, Wesleyan Covenant Association

I've been a lead pastor for over 30 years and have been involved in many staff hirings. *How to Find the Right Pastor* is a resource I wish had been in print three decades ago.

Dr. Jeff Manning
Lead Pastor, Unity Church, Greenville, North Carolina

The process of seeking and calling a new pastor is one of the most challenging "roads" that a church will ever find itself traveling. In *How to Find the Right Pastor*, Ron Hunter and David Gibbs lay out the perfect "roadmap" for successfully navigating this often-treacherous journey from beginning to end. Well organized, concise, and yet comprehensive, I can't recommend this book enough for any pastoral search committee as they embark on their task of calling a new pastor.

Jim Lemons, Ph.D.
Professor of Theological Studies and Leadership
Director, Master of Arts in Theological Studies, Dallas Baptist University

How to Find the Right Pastor **is the most thorough work on this subject that I have ever read. Ron Hunter Jr. and David Gibbs III have done an invaluable service to our churches by writing this easy-to-read, "A to Z" tutorial on this extremely important subject. Mandatory reading for every church leader in America!**

Jim McComas
Executive Director/CEO, Free Will Baptist Family Ministries, Greeneville, Tennessee

This book provides a biblical approach and priceless information emphasizing the importance of prayer in the search journey for God's appointed person—the right pastor for your church.

Mary Lou Hendry
Director, Sanctity of Human Life, Lakeland, Florida
Director, One More Child, Lakeland, Florida

A powder keg, with fuse intact, seems to come packaged with the process of choosing a new pastor. The search committee is handed a book of matches, while the church holds its breath. I highly recommend every church and search committee hold this book instead. David Gibbs and Ron Hunter have written a guidebook, based on years of practical wisdom and experience. Their guidance will defuse the process, saving the candidate, the committee, and the church from imminent danger.

Dr. Stephen Davey
Pastor/Teacher, The Shepherd's Church, Cary, North Carolina
President, Shepherds Theological Seminary, Cary, North Carolina

This invaluable resource offers practical insights and expert advice to help your search committee make a wise and informed decision. Whether you're just beginning the search or narrowing down top candidates, this book provides valuable tools and strategies to ensure a successful outcome.

Dr. Robert J. Pacienza
Senior Pastor, Coral Ridge Presbyterian Church, Fort Lauderdale, Florida

Dr. Hunter and Attorney Gibbs included and discussed the vital selection of an interim pastor. They bring to the forefront numerous overlooked items for search committees to consider.

Edward Moody, Ph.D.
Executive Secretary of National Association of Free Will Baptists
Author of the *First Aid* counseling book series.

Ron Hunter and David Gibbs provide a wise, biblical, and practical step-by-step journey for helping churches meet one of their greatest needs: a pastoral leader who fits their congregation, culture, and community. As a pastor who has recently walked through an intensive pastoral search process, this book will not only serve as a helpful roadmap for search teams and church leaders, but will also benefit the candidates themselves who are making the life-changing decision of where to serve for the next chapter of their ministry.

Jay Strother, D.Ed.Min.
Senior Pastor, Brentwood Baptist Church, Brentwood, Tennessee

Search committees are filled with solid Christian leaders who genuinely don't know where, or how, to begin their work. Now they will. *How to Find the Right Pastor* will be "that book" that will be in the library of every church and Christian organization for a long time to come.

Phil Miller
Director, Center for Church Health
Texas Baptists

No decision more directly impacts a congregation, the families within it, and the community around it, than the pastoral search process. Read this book now, then put it on your shelf for the next time you are in a pastoral call process, or when someone asks you for advice. There is no "magic bullet" for finding the right pastor, but embracing an approach that includes an honest look at your congregation and its leadership will bring benefits far beyond finding the right shepherd.

Wade Mobley, Ph.D.
President of Free Lutheran Seminary and Bible College

How to Find the Right Pastor **is invaluable! Every church should have this book in their library for when the time comes.**

Dr. Frank Harber
President and Chief Legal Counsel, Defending The Faith Alliance

Hunter and Gibbs have created a pragmatic and thorough guide to help a congregation walk through the difficult process resulting from a change of pastors. Each chapter clearly and concisely defines an area that is essential in the process of this change—whether the change is healthy or not. I am impressed both with the thoroughness of the material and with the ease of reading.

Michael Swiger
Executive Director, True Freedom Ministries, Cleveland, Ohio

Dr. Ron Hunter and Attorney David Gibbs III have masterfully simplified an otherwise complicated process. This comprehensive handbook provides a much-needed strategic roadmap for pastoral search committees as they embark on the time-sensitive and emotional process of finding a new pastor.

Rev. Steven M. Baran
President, National Christian Counselors Association, Sarasota, Florida

Sadly, we live in a time that pastoral transition and disqualifications leave many churches void of leadership. This work is clear and concise, yet rich and deep, making a relatively complex task seem manageable.

Kevin M. Jones, Ph.D.
Dean and Assistant Professor, Cedarville University

How to Find the Right Pastor **helps reduce anxiety during transitional periods between pastors. The book's process reduces some of the anxiety as its comprehensive scope pushes you to ask the right questions in any church context.**

Barry Raper, D.Min.
Associate Dean, Welch Divinity School
Pastor, Bethel Free Will Baptist Church

Perhaps no greater decision confronts a church than the selection of their pastor. Many churches don't even know where to begin the process, but great care must be taken in determining who will shepherd the flock as the one charged with "watching for their souls." This book is an invaluable resource for deacons, pulpit committees, and congregations to safeguard their efforts.

Kelly McInerney
Pastor, Bible Baptist Church, Savannah, Georgia

In the days in which we live, David and Ron draw upon their combined experience to provide a detailed and practical roadmap for Bible-believing churches to follow as they seek the senior pastor God has to lead them.

Pastor Dennis W. Jennings
Vice President, Baptist Church Ministry Network

The need for the "right" pastor or staff to lead a church cannot be overstated! *How to Find the Right Pastor* is an invaluable tool that can lessen the intimidation of this important task.

Mason Polk
Director of Institutional Advancement, Randall University

Hunter and Gibbs provide a pointed, honest perspective on this critical process in the life of a church. Every church search committee should prayerfully work through this guide before hiring another pastor.

William Slater
Dean of Adult and Online Studies, Welch College, Gallatin, Tennessee
Tennessee State Representative

The clear, step-by-step process in this book will help our search committees know how to get started right to proceed in a mutually understandable process. This book will help our churches truly find the right pastor and will be the standard for best practices with our pastor-search committees.

Dr. Bruce McCoy
Author of *The Reluctant Peacemaker*
Baptist General Convention of Texas, Dallas, Texas

***How to Find the Right Pastor* is a much-needed resource for churches and especially helpful for pastoral search committees. It also helps you avoid costly mistakes. One of the real gems of this book is the section on building your profile before beginning your search.**

Jonathan Denton, Ph.D.
Associate Professor of Christian Studies/Student Ministry
Charleston Southern University

This book contains incredible advice and biblical strategies to any church committee to find the right pastor for their church. The five phases laid out in the book are concise and compelling tools for finding God's man for your church.

Dr. Eric Capaci
Pastor, Gospel Light Baptist Church, Hot Spring, Arkansas
President, Champion Christian College, Hot Springs, Arkansas

Concise, adaptable, timely, and weighty, describe this handbook. The combination of David C. Gibbs III and Ron Hunter Jr., embraces years of experience from valued and distinctive perspectives. I highly recommend this resource for pastors, boards, and ministry leaders who want to extend legacy and wisely steward any season of transition for the Kingdom's sake.

Rev. Frank Cantadore
Board President, Association of Christian Teachers and Schools
Head of School, Concord Academy, Concord, North Carolina

Personally witnessing the trial and error other churches have gone through in hiring pastors, it's with my highest recommendation that search committees read this comprehensive, practical, and biblical resource prior to the process of finding the right pastor for their congregation.

Walter Colace
Founding/Senior Pastor, Christ Community Church of Imperial Valley

Since everything rises and falls on leadership, you must prepare for these crucial conversations. This amazing book prepares leaders as well as the church, school, or ministry to hire right. As you are well aware, there are no do-overs in these critical searches. The five carefully crafted sections allow you to distinguish between emotional decisions and reality.

Dr. Jay Strack
President and Founder
Student Leadership University

Selections of this magnitude need processes and guardrails. *How to Find the Right Pastor* provides both!

Joe Turner
President & Chief Executive Officer, Ministry Partners Investment Company

TABLE OF CONTENTS

Introduction

"NOT ANOTHER SEARCH COMMITTEE MEETING! We have to fill this position, and we have to fill it now! Quickly! The congregation is getting restless, and some families have already left the church while others are threatening to go. My family wants all this search committee work finished already. I am not thrilled with the candidates we have, but we aren't getting any new ones. Maybe it's God's will for me to ignore my better instincts and just select someone—anyone. What's the worst thing that could happen? Can it be any worse than what we have happening now?"

We understand your frustration, but don't rush this process! Too many pastoral or staff selections have been made based on what the search committee finally decided was "adequate" due diligence, only to realize six months later that slowing down and taking further steps would have been a much better option. Now many of these "short-cut" committees need to begin a new search all over again.

REMEMBER THIS: If you only take one lesson away from this entire handbook, please do not miss this first truth: **NOBODY IS ALWAYS BETTER THAN THE WRONG SOMEBODY!** "Nobody" will ever embezzle money from the ministry, abuse a child in Sunday School or youth group, split the church, change the church's theology and beliefs, or destroy the church! Tragically, the wrong "somebody" could potentially do all of that and so much more to hurt the work of the Lord.

As you approach this most important task of finding a new pastor, recognize that your overarching goal is to find the right "somebody" who will maximize the ministry of your church and minimize unnecessary hurt and liability.

You feel the pressure. We know. But take a deep breath and realize that finding the right person for your church requires patience and much prayer so you can keep in sync with the leading of the Lord. Just as Luke 14:28 counsels, if you start building a house or if you launch a business with no plans, you will not efficiently and effectively achieve your goal of a solid house or a successful business. While we understand that such diligence is necessary in our daily lives, when it comes to the church, we must be at least as diligent. We can't throw caution to the wind and just hope for the best.

Churches searching for a pastor should have a definitive process for doing so. Resist making a hasty selection about "who" without first doing the homework of deciding "what" you are looking for.

Just as pastors have distinct personalities, so do congregations. Many mismatches have caused major frustrations and hurt for both sides of this spiritual equation. But taking the time to find a healthy fit requires more effort than some churches are willing to put into the process. Because the hiring processes of a typical company's human resources department may not fit a ministry's goals, the methodology of searching for a pastor may also be unfamiliar to even professionals in the congregation.

Finding a high-capacity candidate isn't terribly difficult, but does that person's chemistry fit with your particular congregation? Many search committees do not know how to detect such nuances that could cause problems later on in the church.

The following chapters help you navigate through the categories your search committee will need to wrestle with to find just the right pastor for your church. Such categories include biblical criteria, educational expectations, geographical predispositions, work and ministry experience, spouse expectations, kid-related issues, involvement within the church leadership, social organizations, political involvement, and much more.

Because you must consider so many variables in your search, the process can get overwhelming. This book lays out an easy-to-follow search process with coaching provided at each step along the way—plus forms to help you compare the most important criteria among your potential candidates.

Consider the FBI behavioral analysis unit. When solving a crime, the FBI observes clues and creates a profile that describes in detail the suspect's traits and characteristics. This profile includes things such as a suspect's general age, socio-economic background, education level, childhood history, and their likely habits. The many details they are looking for in a suspect help them build a suspect profile, all without having a name.

Those congregations that take the time to first do a fair assessment of their church and then build a pastor profile to measure their candidates will have a decisive advantage in finding a long-term healthy fit for the congregation. This book will guide you to build a profile of "what" you are looking for, with all the desired traits, before you ever look at a single résumé or candidate questionnaire. Once the church assessment and pastor profile are complete, the selection process will become much more straightforward. The more time spent crafting the profile, the less time the search committee will agonize over hard choices.

This book covers five sections, one for each of the five vital steps needed in your search.

The **first section** helps you ***Prepare for Your Search*** by analyzing your church, forming the search committee, and finding an interim—all before interviewing potential candidates—to ensure your church is ready for the next steps.

The **second section** helps the search committee begin ***Building Your Pastoral Profile*** of characteristics your church will want and need in its next pastor, which will provide a matrix upon which all candidates will be evaluated.

The **third section** assists the committee in ***Finding and Narrowing to Your Top 3 to 5 Candidates.*** Most search committees start at step three, which hinders their selection process.

The **fourth section** provides you with tools to conduct ***First Interviews With Your Top 3 to 5 Candidates*** based upon your defined pastor profile, measuring every candidate in a very objective manner to narrow your list to the one candidate you wish to bring in for a low-key, in-person second interview with your search committee and a visit to your church.

The **fifth section** walks you through the ***Top Candidate Visit and the Vote*** components that bring your top candidate in to meet and preach to the congregation, visit with various groups in the church, and participate in a churchwide question-and-answer session, all of which ends in a vote on whether to affirm the candidate as your new pastor.

The appendix provides forms, questionnaires, examples, and other resources (all downloadable at FindPastor.com).

Divided into short chapters, this handbook forms a true reference book to help you find the needed information quickly. While it is recommended that you read the entire book before beginning your search, the chapter divisions will allow you to return quickly to each of the specific topics and concerns as they arise during your search process.

This handbook will work well for finding any church staff member, but finding a pastor is always the most difficult and important. Finding the right type of spiritual leader for you and your family and your church is far more involved and a much more serious process than simply hiring a clerk for a convenience store. If you put in the necessary prayer, dedication, and hard work, you will find great satisfaction in what you accomplish for your church and for the Lord. Roll up your sleeves; it is time to do the hard work of finding and keeping your next pastor.

SECTION 1

Preparing for Your Search

1

Avoiding Fatal Scenarios

While some pastors will stay at one church for decades or even their entire career, if your church finds itself looking for a pastor every three or four years, you're not alone. In fact, you're among the average. But it doesn't have to stay this way. Increasing the service longevity of the pastors your church chooses may just be a matter of improving your pastoral search process.

Putting this book in the hands of church search committee members will save churches thousands of dollars, countless time, and a great deal of frustration.

An all-too-familiar scenario:

> We welcomed Pastor Mark and his family. He was just what our church needed—or so we thought. After about six months, some of us began to notice a few red flags. Others would not see the issues for another year, but it was obvious that the result of our pastoral search would not and could not be a long-term fit. What started as minor concerns later turned into full-blown issues. Certain age groups felt isolated, ignored, and with no voice. The pastor changed so many things that we hardly recognized our church anymore. What mattered most to us did not seem to matter to our new pastor.

How did the pulpit committee find Mark? Well, someone suggested him, and we started with a phone interview. Mark made a great impression and had a solid résumé. His previous church's website seemed positive and healthy. Every clue he provided indicated we had discovered someone who would fit in with our ministry. We invited him and his family to the church for a meet-and-greet, a "trial sermon," and a basic question-and-answer period, where he handled each question with passion and insight. If only we had known what questions needed to be asked at that time.

In hindsight, Mark had probably preached his all-time best sermon that day, but we should have explored his historical preaching content from the past couple of years. The biggest miss was not knowing what questions to ask of him and others before inviting him to come and meet the church. It's no wonder our search ultimately failed; we apparently didn't know how to evaluate candidates properly.

Another scenario:

Mark just resigned, and the police are asking us, "Did you do a background check before you hired him?" A teenage girl in the church is posting online that she and Mark are "in love" and are having an "affair." The sex crime detectives are asking where they can find Mark to interview him.

The church treasurer is also trying to understand what happened. Apparently, our church missionaries are saying they haven't received any support from the church for months. Upon investigation, the mission funds appear to have been paying for some personal credit cards used by Mark's wife and children. Upon his resignation, Mark's last words to our board president were, "You didn't pay me enough, so go to the police if you want to, but they won't do anything about it because you and the treasurer let it happen."

Even if your pastoral experience is less dramatic than the above scenarios, if you find yourself seeking a pastor, your entire search committee should read this handbook. **The table of contents will work like an index, helping you quickly find any information.** Combine the insights of this book with committee prayers for discernment, and your outcomes should start looking very different from the above fatal scenarios.

2

Ordering the Search Process Timeline

Your pastor has left or will soon be leaving your church. So, that position is open or will open soon. What are your next steps? Below is a timeline you can check off as you move through the search process. A short summary of each step follows the checklist.

Timeline Checklist

- ☐ Read This Book
- ☐ Choose Your Search Committee
- ☐ Install an Interim Pastor
- ☐ Develop a Communication Strategy and Schedule
- ☐ Analyze Your Church
- ☐ Build Your Pastor Profile
- ☐ Look for Candidates
- ☐ Pray and Evaluate
- ☐ First Interviews With Your Top 3 to 5 Candidates
- ☐ Low-key Weekend Visit With the Top Candidate
- ☐ Conditional Offer of Employment and Background Checks
- ☐ Announce the Candidate to the Congregation
- ☐ Second Church Visit: Candidate Preaches/Churchwide Q & A
- ☐ Evaluate
- ☐ Final Steps & Vote

READ THIS BOOK – Every member of the leadership board that will select the search committee, any current pastoral staff, and the search committee itself (if it's already chosen), should read this book before beginning the search process.

CHOOSE YOUR SEARCH COMMITTEE – Your first task is to select a search committee. Try to include representatives from as many ages and ministry groups in the church as possible while keeping the total number of committee members to no more than seven to nine. The search committee can be appointed by your church leadership board (perhaps with nominations from the various groups or church members). Or the leadership board can nominate individuals to present to the church membership for a vote. Or your church may already have this aspect of the search process written into its bylaws.

INSTALL AN INTERIM PASTOR – Before beginning the search, the combined leadership board and search committee should determine whether to utilize an interim pastor or whether a current pastoral staff member should fill in as the interim. The advantages and pitfalls of each choice are discussed in this handbook.

DEVELOP A COMMUNICATION STRATEGY AND SCHEDULE – Develop a strategy for how the search committee will communicate to the congregation and to others during the search process. How much will be communicated? In what forum? Emphasize the importance of confidentiality. Make sure that an important part of your communication strategy is prayer—both as a committee and with the congregation—when making reports. Developing a time schedule is also important; however, that schedule should be loosely held and retooled regularly, since you don't really know at this point how long the various elements of the search will actually take.

ANALYZE YOUR CHURCH – Begin the process of objectively evaluating your church. Identify the various stakeholders. What is important to the church? What are its needs? What broader community factors should be considered, such as its atmosphere and its needs that the church might be able to address? What sort of pastor will be needed?

BUILD YOUR PASTOR PROFILE – Once you have assessed your church and its surrounding community, you will be better able to make the list of characteristics you'll want to see in your ideal candidate. The pastor profile will be your guide for screening any candidate and arriving at the one you will announce to the church as your pastoral candidate.

LOOK FOR CANDIDATES – Create a specific window of time to receive résumés and provide a deadline for ending this collection process. However, keep in mind and be open to the fact that God may bring someone to you later in the process. Discuss the various options available to you for finding candidates: seminaries, word of mouth, job posting websites (preferably only those that advertise ministry-related positions), or denominational or faith community resources. Appoint one person on the committee to receive and hold all candidate submissions until reaching the deadline for receiving them. When you have all the candidate résumés and submissions, share them with the entire search committee for the first time.

PRAY AND EVALUATE – After each committee member has reviewed and evaluated all the résumés and submissions, pray for guidance and discuss each candidate. You may, as a group, dismiss some immediately. Other candidates may already stand out as good possibilities. Continue to have your entire committee evaluate those who are not immediately dismissed. After reviewing candidate questionnaires and conducting on-site visits or website visits, compare the top candidates to the pastor profile you have developed and rank the candidates in descending order starting with the person who best seems to match your pastor profile. Then plan to interview your top three to five candidates, beginning with the best match and working down your list.

FIRST INTERVIEWS WITH YOUR TOP 3 TO 5 CANDIDATES – Plan to interview your top three to five candidates either in person or via a web-based video call, depending on distance factors and what would work best for each candidate. Develop a score for each candidate based on the interviews, site visits, websites, sermons, and other interactions or information. **Always score based on your pastor profile.** Determine the strengths and weaknesses of each candidate. Make this a serious matter of prayer, asking God to help you choose the best candidate for your church as you continue with the process.

LOW-KEY WEEKEND VISIT WITH THE TOP CANDIDATE – Invite your top candidate (with spouse or alone) to visit your church for a weekend. The candidate can see the church, look at the area, evaluate the local schools, and get a "feel" for the church and the community. This visit would also be the time for the search committee's second interview, this time in-person in a more personal and casual setting. This second interview will also be the time to begin discussing practical considerations, such as salary, benefits, work expectations, and other "housekeeping" items to make sure that both your committee and the candidate are on the same page regarding these areas. What does the church expect from the pastor? What does the pastor expect from the church? Explore both of these questions in depth, so the big issues are settled if the candidate is presented to the church for a vote.

CONDITIONAL OFFER OF EMPLOYMENT AND BACKGROUND CHECKS – If, after the weekend visit, your top candidate is still your top candidate and this person still wants to move forward pursuing the pastoral opportunity, the church is now ready to make a conditional offer of employment. This step means informing the candidate that the church intends to hire pending approval from the church (either the congregation or the leadership board—or whatever other approval method is set forth in the church bylaws) and acceptable background checks. Once this conditional offer has been made, obtain written approval from the candidate to do a credit check and a criminal background check. Some churches have been very surprised to learn at this point that the person they were considering has a sordid or checkered background, so don't skip this part! By completing your conditional offer of employment, you ensure the candidate will accept the terms and benefits before involving the entire church and getting everyone's hopes falsely raised.

ANNOUNCE THE CANDIDATE TO THE CONGREGATION – Assuming this candidate passes the credit and background checks and accepts the conditional employment offer, it is time to announce the candidate to the church. Inform the congregation by having the candidate record a video to be shown in the church service or simply by having the chair of the search committee introduce and describe the candidate during a church service while displaying a photo of the candidate with the candidate's family on a large screen. Explain to those in the service (and in a follow-up email to your congregation so those who may have missed the service are not left in the dark) the steps the church has taken to get to this point and what the next steps will be.

SECOND CHURCH VISIT: CANDIDATE PREACHES/ CHURCHWIDE Q & A – Have the candidate come back for another weekend visit within a week or two of announcing the candidacy to the church. The goal of this weekend is to have the church family get to know the candidate and the candidate's family (and vice versa). Schedule the candidate to preach at least one sermon and to be available for a meet and greet and a question/answer session with the congregation. Also plan and schedule for this weekend to be a time of interaction with various church groups (if applicable) and leaders so the visit can be the most informative for both the candidate and the congregation.

EVALUATE – Following this weekend visit, plan a congregational townhall-style feedback session to invite honest impressions. Begin with prayer for guidance and allow everyone to freely express both positive and negative reactions. Don't try to justify the committee's decision or to force acceptance of the candidate. But if all lights appear to be green, the search committee is ready to declare that the candidate will be voted upon by the congregation (or whatever process the bylaws require). Be sure to leave this meeting letting the congregation know that the leadership board and search committee are available to answer or discuss any further questions and concerns they may have.

FINAL STEPS & VOTE – Assuming a general positive consensus still exists, plan to have the church vote on the candidate two to three weeks after the candidate's preaching weekend (most church bylaws require providing the congregation at least a two-week notice after the candidate preaches prior to voting). This time gives people a chance to pray about the candidate and how they will vote, time to listen or watch the candidate's available online sermons (if any), discuss the candidate with family and friends, rearrange schedules so they can be available to vote, and ask further questions of the leadership board and search committee as necessary.

By the time the church votes on whether to call this candidate as their pastor, the search committee should be fairly certain of how the vote will turn out, and the candidate should be pretty clear about accepting the call if the final vote is favorable. Notify the candidate of the results of the vote soon after the results are tallied. The candidate should know ahead of time what percentage is necessary to be approved. Some church bylaws only require a majority while others require 90 or 95 percent.

If the vote is favorable, the candidate may decide to accept the offer immediately or may take some time to consider the results of the vote (extra time might be especially true if only a majority is needed and the vote barely reached a majority, as the candidate may not feel that scenario will be a very welcoming one). If the candidate verbally agrees to accept the vote and the call to the church, inform the church members as soon as possible; email is preferable if the church won't be meeting together for another week. The church and the candidate will then formalize the agreement with an employment contract.

IF NO? – If the congregational vote to call the candidate as pastor is negative, or the candidate had a change of heart after interacting with the entire church, or if the vote total is not acceptable to the candidate, the search committee should then move on to the next candidate on the top three to five list and repeat the process from that step forward.

3

Praying Through the Process

We all believe in prayer. Most lost people even believe in prayer, especially in crisis situations. But do we actually pray? That is a different question.

Ask yourself honestly: did the leadership group that selected (or recommended) your search committee members get together to pray for God's guidance in making those choices? And has your search committee gotten together and spent even 30 minutes together in prayer? A half hour is the length of a standard television show or video download, but often, we are "too busy" or to focused on the practical aspects of the search committee to bring God and prayer regularly into the process.

You can get every detail right and even vote on the perceived "best" candidate, but if you leave prayer out of the process, you could be starting over again in just a couple of years. A biblical reminder of this pitfall comes from the selection of the first two kings of Israel: Saul and David.

You know the story. The Israelites created a profile of what sort of king they wanted, but their criteria were shallow and lacked the characteristics of a true leader. When seeking their first king, Israel merely desired what other nations had instead of seeking what they really needed. They first selected a tall, strong, handsome, kingly-looking leader with Saul.

But when seeking their second king, the people trusted their prophet Samuel, who first sought and heard from God before looking to where God was leading him. Coming to Jesse's home, Samuel asked to see all his sons. He looked them over carefully from oldest to youngest, thinking the older and stronger son would be "the one." Thankfully, while evaluating each of the brothers, Samuel was still praying AND listening to God. God was saying, "Not the one." Then when standing in front of the youngest, the smallest, and the child with the least experience, God told the selection committee (Samuel), not to look on the outside, but on the heart, because David was the one.

You will search for the best pastor, of course, not ignoring those obvious traits that typically result in optimum outcomes. But when you lean on God, praying consistently, you may find a candidate with greater potential than experience.

The rest of this handbook will help you discover the important criteria you should consider with God's leading. Your job will then be to help your congregation see and agree to what truly matters. As you pray, also share verses among yourselves (and possibly with the congregation) to reinforce your posture of seeking God's choice over your own.

Claim the promise so clearly given in the book of James that says if any lack wisdom, they can admit that lack and totally depend on God in prayer. He always promises to give abundantly beyond what we can ask or think in our own human condition.

It is an awesome thought to recognize that God owns the church, God loves the church, Christ died for the church, and we (you!) now have the privilege of doing the very work of God! We most certainly need to admit our limits as mere mortals and put our faith in total dependence on the Almighty!

Prayer, like a new eyeglass prescription, allows you to clearly see the details others might miss. Prayer provides the lens through which you should view the search process, the other committee members, the church, and the candidates themselves.

Do not forget to pray about your attitude. If your prayers sound like a search committee of one, then you may want to either remove yourself from the committee or pray to be a more healthy and collaborative part of the team. No one prays the following out loud, "My will God, not yours," which you would acknowledge is dangerously unobjective.

Take ten minutes as a committee to confess together before the Lord. Confession can be healthy and humbling. Then take ten minutes to adore and thank the Lord for all the blessings He provides. Finally, take ten minutes to petition and ask Him to meet the needs of the church and the committee.

As you petition the Lord, pray for your heart to be ready to go where God wants to take you. Pray for discerning insight as you sort through the desired traits needed in your next pastor. Pray that you focus on what *could be* rather than on what *has been*. Pray for patience. Pray for God's power in the church during the transition.

When praying, seek God's choice over yours. Do not ask God to make the other search committee members see all the great attributes in your favorite candidate. Pray for spiritual objectivity and discernment. Ask God to help you discern the candidates' true character, integrity, and capability.

Pray earnestly when analyzing your church and the target profile for the new pastor. Pray that the profile will show precisely what the church needs and what God desires. Pray for honest, open discussion from all search committee members. Pray for mutual respect to be a high priority among the search team as various opinions may conflict with others.

Prayer has a way of allowing you to see beyond the obvious. Your search committee should pray and function in the same way Samuel searched for King David and not the way the people desired Saul. Getting your hearts aligned in prayer will allow you to look discerningly at the candidates' hearts. Praying with the candidates themselves during the interview process is also a strongly recommended practice.

4

Recovering From Losing Your Pastor

Change is difficult. People grow comfortable with how things are, and living through change is an inherently unsettling process. Plus, churches are traditional organizations that often worry change will lead to unhealthy compromises or outright carnality. Change can also be painful, and being aware of how people in the church are hurting through the change process is important.

One of two scenarios likely unfolded to cause you to read this book. In the first scenario, the congregation regrets the departure of your long- or short-time pastor. You will deeply miss the vision, leadership, sermons, and personal touches. Your pastor may be stepping down for personal reasons, relocating to another position, or retiring, and you wonder how in the world you will ever find another pastor this great. The daunting task and impending search may make you wonder if it can ever be this good again.

The second scenario may occur more often than the first. Your pastor is leaving, and it may not be a day too soon. You have been waiting for this day, having recognized early on it was a bad fit—a mismatch evidenced by personality clashes and ineffectiveness. A lack of support from the membership or even an impending split may indicate this day is long overdue.

In either scenario, some people will be excited about the possibility of a fresh face while others will mourn the loss of a genuine connection. When a pastor leaves, emotions range from excitement to anxiety. Sadly, in many cases, if a spiritual forensics team came in to investigate, the chalked outlines of the fallen would reveal more victims than expected. In addition to members, attendees, and the former pastor, the biggest victim may be the church's unity and future direction. Many congregations have fractured or lost membership over pastoral or other key staffing changes.

When the church loses a pastor, emotions run high. Much like at the end of a championship game, part of the crowd will celebrate, and part will mourn. Both groups invested some degree of sweat, work, and emotion into the relationship. Everyone will feel drained and will need recovery time. Open and honest dialogue with key leaders (volunteers and staff), and perhaps even the congregation, will likely reveal that each "team on the field" (pastor and church) made mistakes. Like a great coach, it's important to take time to analyze the team's successes (what went right) and the team's failures (what went wrong) so they will be better prepared for the future.

Allowing open and honest dialogue, while perhaps painful, will help rebuild trust and heal wounds from the loss of a pastor, which will in turn minimize the risk of future church fractures. Healing begins with listening to everyone's thoughts and concerns. Only when the staff and congregation believe their views and concerns are understood and will be considered will you (and they) be ready to start the search process. Prepare a time to hear what the people want and do not want in their next pastor—without throwing the previous pastor under the bus. To get broad buy-in, provide convenient opportunities for various groups within the church to provide input, or (better yet) allow everyone that same opportunity if the congregation's size permits. Being receptive to input and feedback in this manner will not only build trust and begin to heal hurts, but it will also go a long way toward helping the search committee build a profile sheet for the next pastor.

If there are no immoral or illegal reasons for your pastor's leaving, take time to honor and recognize the pastor's tenure, even if a large group is happy about the pastor's exit. Making sure to honor the pastor's departure with a gift or social time or special recognition during a service will emphasize the positive and pare down the negative. Emphasizing positive experiences and contributions can also help dispel accusations or rumors.

Recognition brings closure and appropriate honor, whether for much or for little, in the same way that a funeral helps family members adjust to a loss. Like at a funeral, people know the good and the bad, but why focus on the failures? A leader in the congregation should be able to highlight particular accomplishments of the pastor's leadership. You can never go wrong publicly honoring the successes no matter how few or insignificant, but quiet informal conclaves of pastor-bashing will leave scars on the next generation and are likely to cause further division in the church. Show young believers how to honor and respect the shepherd's role even in disagreement.

Regardless of the reasons, a pastor's departure will cause wounds. If the pastor leaves due to an affair, embezzlement, bad ethical choices, or other forms of immorality, the church will be left feeling angry, deceived, manipulated, and very hurt. Even having a pastor leave to take a bigger church can result in feelings of inferiority and a sense of loss for a congregation. In today's climate, the church needs to own and communicate the reality of the situation and the why behind the departure. Unexplained hasty departures tend to cause later disruptions for seemingly insignificant reasons. In such circumstances, there needs to be tactful honesty without spelling out all the sordid details.

Healing the wounds left behind is not the responsibility of the departing pastor. Healing occurs when the hurting patient decides to accept treatment, which can only begin by looking forward rather than dwelling in the past. Some congregations cannot grow because they think their best days are in the past. Others cannot succeed because they keep reopening old wounds. If you have open wounds in the church, building trust and healing those wounds is vital. Encourage forgiveness. Invest significant time in prayer, asking God what *He* wants to do with the church's future rather than deciding *for* Him what should be done. Encourage your church to look to the future by praying and trusting the Lord to bring *His* choice for the pastor who will be most effective at reaching the next generation. Praying together tears down walls, builds community, and heals hurts.

As it is commonly said, "Hurting people hurt people and are easily hurt by them." A congregation that's been hurt by a previous pastor or staff member's departure may, even unintentionally, hurt their new pastor, who may in turn, reflect those same actions or feelings toward the flock, leading to a vicious cycle that never ends well. Prayer and forgiveness that occurs *before* the new pastor is chosen will allow the congregation's wounds to heal so the church can become healthy and ready to take on the search challenge. Admit that wounds exist and identify what caused them. But then build trust by facilitating an environment of openness, healing, reconciliation, and forgiveness.

5

Forming the Search Committee

The search committee undertakes a role of paramount importance. To say its members hold unwritten history in their hands is an understatement. They are literally taking assets and opportunities given to the church by God Himself and deciding who will best steward those resources.

Any who fail to understand the significance of their role, or take it too lightly, or do it for the wrong reasons are being derelict before God Himself. Who will reach, disciple, and baptize your children and grandchildren? Who will perform pre-marital counseling and wedding ceremonies? Who will speak final words over your loved ones and possibly even you? Who will be responsible to bring in staff members and volunteers who will shape your children's and even your own worldview? Who will facilitate the spiritual formation of your members, the widows, singles, and others in your church families as they grow from generation to generation? Who will steer the vision of the congregation?

While the pastor does not always have direct contact with every area of the church, every area is affected by the actions of that office and role. It is therefore so important to have a search committee that truly represents every major area of your church—and every individual in your church.

The following are some of the most common questions and answers we've received about search committees:

1. Can the search committee consist of everyone in the congregation?

   No. It would not be practical or productive to do so, even if your church is extremely small.

2. Can you have a representative from every ministry in the church?

   This is also probably not practical if you have numerous ministries, although the goal should be to have as many age groups and ministries as possible represented in some capacity, keeping in mind that most search committee members could represent more than one area of the church. Consider including one trusted older teenager who understands confidentiality to sit on the search committee. Teenagers can add a fresh perspective and insight that might otherwise be lacking on the committee.

   Once the search gets underway, be careful that the search committee members are not so pragmatic in their search that they look only to the interests of their own groups and fail to protect the highest priorities on the pastor profile.

3. Can our church leadership board also be the search committee?

   Your leadership board may already have the appropriate makeup to serve as the search committee. Sometimes, the leadership board consists of representatives from the major areas of the church's ministries along with a congregational member at-large. However, for the average church, the leadership board is likely to be five to seven older men who may have forgotten how parents of small kids think and who don't understand what single parents or widows deal with. Such a board is also likely to be lacking a female or youth perspective. In that case, the leadership board should nominate or perhaps even directly select church members to the search committee who will add a varied perspective.

Hopefully your leadership board is made up of godly individuals who seek God's agenda for the church and not their own and who look out for the good of the entire congregation and not just any one age group. If so, your board's wisdom and years of experience should produce a balanced search committee that will derail any who might try to sway the search process by emotion or only short-term considerations.

4. What are the possibilities for the makeup of a strong search committee?

   Your search committee could be comprised of your leadership board plus some additional members from unrepresented age groups and church ministries. Or it could be a completely unique committee chosen by the board or members to represent the various age groups and ministries in the church—resulting in a healthy representative group dynamic. Or, particularly in very large churches with many staff members, the search committee might consist primarily of current staff members who will need to bring in someone they trust and can work with.

5. Should the opinions of paid staff (or anyone else!) hold greater weight on the search committee than the opinions of other committee members?

No. Heavier weight should not be put on the opinions of one person over another. Remember that everyone (including paid staff) should feel represented on the committee, but this representation is undermined if, for example, the younger representatives' opinions or insights are dismissed outright because they are different from that of the deacon who's been there for 40 years. Allowing everyone on the committee equal consideration and a forum that allows them to freely express their thoughts and provide input to other committee members will build trust between the committee, the remaining staff, and the congregation as the search process unfolds.

When each committee member truly seeks God's heart and direction in the search process, none of them will seek to be the committee "star." Finding the right pastor must override any search committee member dominating the process. The search process should focus on the future of the church by finding a pastor who will bring God glory rather than bringing glory to any one age, group, or person.

6. How many people should be on the search committee?

Making room for every age group and church ministry to be represented on the search committee could result in a fairly large group. To avoid that result, find people who could represent the perspective of multiple areas and ages in the church. For instance, a mom who has a teenager and an elementary-age child could represent women's, youth, and children's ministries all at the same time. A good rule of thumb regarding numbers is to stay around seven to nine committee members—certainly not much higher.

The committee should not be so large that its members feel uneasy sharing honest opinions and feedback. In a much larger group, typically only a small percentage of the committee will feel comfortable sharing critical or affirming comments about issues or people. You need a group small enough to build consensus but not too large to become unwieldy.

7. What expectations should we have of the search committee members?

   All members of the committee should be financially supporting the church. To allow a non-donor to serve on this committee would be a mistake because they have no financial stake in the outcome.

   All members of the committee should fully disclose any potential conflicts of interest to the other committee members. Such conflicts would include any potential or actual financial or personal relationships the committee member has with any potential candidates or the ministry from which a candidate comes (if applicable).

   All members of the committee should commit to dedicating the time necessary to the process. If they cannot attend meetings due to work, travel, health, or other reasons, they should decline to serve.

   All members of the committee should agree to confidentiality. The work of the committee should not be subject to outside pressure, online disclosure, or gossip. This committee needs to agree not to leak details but to speak publicly with one voice in a spirit of unity.

   All members of the committee should lovingly submit to each other in a spirit of humility, cooperation, and accountability. The members should be slow to offend and quick to forgive as they share and work together.

All members of the committee need to realize that serving on this committee cannot replace their personal walk with God. Doing the work of the Lord is not a replacement for being a man or woman of God. Prayer and time in the Bible are extra important as you undertake this spiritual work for your church.

Count it an honor to serve on the search committee. Pray, participate, and evaluate, knowing your decisions affect generations in the church. Most of all, seek the correct candite, not your favorite candidate.

6

Budgeting for Your Search

Jesus talked frequently about the topic of money. Approximately 15% of His sermons and 25% of His parables addressed financial issues. The Bible has 2,300 verses about money and possessions, which is even more than the number of verses about salvation.

The love of money is evil, but the proper stewardship of money for God's work will be blessed abundantly. If you want to quickly evaluate a person's priorities, their bank and credit card statements are a good place to start (but we're not suggesting you ask your candidates for bank or credit card statements!).

The costs of a thorough pastoral search are not insignificant, but they are manageable. As in many areas of life, you get what you pay for, and this is not the moment to expend as few resources as possible. Being cheap will likely cost the church a lot more than just finances in the long run.

Common concerns about finances when a pastor leaves include funding the day-to-day activities the pastor would have normally handled plus paying for the costs of the search for a new person. Both the mundane internal church tasks and the new search committee tasks will require funds, with the largest expense being time. How does a congregation deal with all these new costs and responsibilities?

After a pastor's departure, church leaders quickly discover the mountain of mundane tasks the pastor handled. Some of those ordinary routines must continue despite the pastor's absence. If you have other staff or administrative assistants, they can keep sorting mail, turning on the heat or air in preparation for services, ordering supplies, ensuring small group and Sunday School curriculum gets ordered, flushing toilets after services, and many other tasks. But what about the relational tasks such as preaching, counseling, training, greeting, recruiting, and meeting with committees? You may need an interim pastor or consultant to help, and that person will need to be paid.

If the church has no staff members beyond the pastor, you will need to recruit competent church members to handle the routine, non-relational tasks. Remember the old proverb, "Many hands make light work?" Seek out several capable volunteers who would be willing and would desire to help share the load. Make a list of necessary tasks and match the right volunteers with the appropriate duties. Spreading the functions among many volunteers removes the risk of asking too much from any one person. Volunteering gives people purpose even in the smallest tasks, and it also gives them an appreciation for all the pastor regularly did.

Consider tasking one group to oversee the administrative details. The church board, trustees, leadership council, or an ad-hoc group could make sure each task is assigned, whether to volunteers or other staff members, and can be available to answer questions and ensure nothing major is overlooked. You will obviously miss some things, but don't over-stress about it; adjust and learn, then regroup. Bills still need to be paid, missionaries still need to be supported, and the lights need to stay on!

An interim pastor will likely be needed to fill the more relational tasks, and the interim pastor needs to be paid appropriately. The role and duties of interims fit somewhere on a sliding scale, from preaching only Sunday sermons, to serving as the temporary pastor, to helping with all the normal pastoral duties. A trusted interim pastor can provide healthy counsel, healing, and lay the groundwork for the new pastor.

Even if the interim only preaches on Sundays, you should value their preparation time, which is much greater than the time it takes to deliver a sermon. Most pastors spend several hours of preparation time for each sermon in Bible study, exposition of Scripture, and any slide designs. Their pay should not be set only for the 30 to 60 minutes of visible work, but also for their expertise, preparation, sacrifice, and the body of work that brought them to you.

The costs of this position need not be equal to the whole salary of a lead pastor, which will give you some savings that can be applied toward your pastoral search. If the committee works the search intentionally and without rushing, the church might actually be able to bank some surplus over the three to twelve months it will likely take to find a new pastor.

Aside from paying the interim pastor, the committee will likely spend little to no money on the search process itself until the best three to five candidates are determined. Funds should then cover travel expenses if the need arises to hear and observe potential candidates in their own setting, to contact references, and to conduct background checks, credit checks, initial interviews, etc. prior to determining and bringing in your top candidate for a second, in-person interview and then the final preaching weekend at your church.

Traveling to the candidates may not be necessary if you do extensive online research on your list of candidates. However, if traveling to hear candidates is determined to be necessary, the church should pay normal travel expenses for those sent. Expenses will include mileage or airfare, hotel, meals, tips, and any other normal, travel-related expenses. Limiting this level of focus to the top three to five candidates will help minimize your costs.

Once you determine which one candidate will be brought in for the second interview and again to preach to your congregation, you will need to pay the expenses for these trips. Provide the candidate and any family with a nice hotel near the church; do not expect them to stay with a family in your church. The candidate and spouse will need time to talk openly without fear of being overheard or misunderstood while processing the possibilities, and they will need time and space to process their meetings and interactions without also having to be a guest in someone's home. Pay the means of transportation that is reasonable. You could expect the family to drive if the trip is under seven to eight hours. Otherwise, plane fare will be essential.

Please do not rush the process. Your committee members as well as the rest of the church will need time to heal, assess, and build your profile. Communicate often and effectively with the entire congregation so they will support the search process. A pastoral search is not free, but few worthwhile things are. Put the time and money into a solid search and watch for God to bless you with a return on your investment.

7

Reasons for and Roles of an Interim Pastor

Pastors leave for a variety of reasons, and the circumstances surrounding their departure—especially their reasons for doing so—generally determine if the departure is healthy or hurtful. Think of the pastor as a cross-country tour bus driver who advances the passengers (the congregation) from one stop to another: informing, guiding, taking on new passengers, and sadly, seeing some get off the bus. Having grown accustomed to the driver's mannerisms, travel insights, and overall care for everyone, changing drivers is, for some, disconcerting and, for others, traumatic.

The tour bus driver analogy helps you understand the two scenarios described: a driver leaves on healthy or hurtful terms. If the driver informs the passengers of the impending changes and shares openly and honestly, people will be saddened by the change, but it will be less hurtful. However, if the driver stole from the bus riders, insulted a rider's spouse, or decided to take half the occupants to another "better bus," the remaining riders will likely transfer a full range of hurtful and negative emotions to the new driver unless the situation is dealt with carefully.

Occasionally, pastors leave a congregation due to their unexpected death or a disabling illness. While dying or developing a chronic illness is no one's choice, the pain is still significant, but it doesn't come with the blame or rancor that other types of departures entail.

On the other hand, churches with a pastor who harmed their congregation in some way may have some members experience a level of post-traumatic stress. Some may even begin to question their faith and their commitment to this church—or to any church.

Bringing in an experienced interim pastor, which will usually be a retired pastor from another church, can be an excellent short-term solution for the church, giving the congregation an opportunity to regroup, begin the healing process, and plan next steps.

The decision of whether to use an interim and the process for selecting one may already be established in the church bylaws. If it isn't, this decision should be made by the church's leadership board. The selection of the interim will encompass some of the same steps as selecting a new pastor, but it does not need to be nearly as extensive since it is a temporary position.

At a minimum, the leadership board needs to make sure that a potential interim has considerable experience leading a church, is aligned with the church's religious beliefs (and, if applicable, denominational distinctives), and has a preaching style and a personal manner that is likely to resonate with the congregation. The board can determine these last two characteristics by watching and listening to past sermons, conducting a thorough, in-person interview of the potential interim, and by checking several personal and professional references. The board will also want to be sure to conduct a criminal background check and a credit check once a conditional offer of employment has been made. Essentially, the board will want to treat the process of selecting an interim as a (much) shorter version of selecting a new pastor.

If the prior pastor has departed in a hurtful manner, whether due to sexual immorality, addictive sin, narcissistic leadership abuse, ethical impropriety, or after having caused a split in the church, the interim's primary job will be to help the congregation heal. Often the latter (a church split) creates longer-lasting congregational wounds than the others, so the interim will have to be especially sensitive to the needs of the congregation under these circumstances.

Returning to our bus analogy, the interim bus driver should be less concerned about charting a new destination for the bus than about treating and helping the traumatized passengers. Changing the bus metaphor a bit, think about if the bus had been in a crash. While a bus crash shakes up all the passengers, the bus riders (church members) closest to the impact will need even more care and time to heal. Helping the church through this process will have to be handled with wisdom, discernment, and patience.

However, suppose the pastor departed on more healthy or pleasant terms. In that case, the interim's role should focus more on keeping the current momentum (kind of business-as-usual) and help prepare everyone for the future transition to a new pastor. The interim bus driver should help the passengers warm up to the idea of having a new person at the wheel. The interim should not plot new directions or stops but should stay on the main roads as prescribed until the new driver can determine if a course change is warranted.

While not charged with going in an entirely new direction, the interim bus driver should always help conduct any much-needed maintenance on the bus. Proper care and attention to neglected areas will allow the new driver to focus on what matters rather than on the tyranny of the urgent. In addition to fixing the bus, the interim can address any unhealthy cultures on the bus. No one wants to ride a bus with a gang any more than people want to attend a church that is controlled by one family or group. Interims know their time is limited, so they can more easily tackle such challenging issues without fear of being fired from their career position. The interim pastor should advise the congregation on ways to get healthier, making the role of the new pastor a bit easier.

Just as the church should provide a job description for its long-term hire (discussed later in this handbook), it should also provide one for the interim, recognizing that adjustments might be needed as the interim becomes more familiar with the congregation. The job description might only anticipate preaching during specified services, but it also could include other expectations: participating in all or part of weekly activities, counseling, hospital visitation, elder care, administering ordinances, performing weddings, and conducting funerals. Interims can also be invaluable in providing counsel and leadership for deacon, trustee, or other board meetings. Smaller congregations may consider a layperson leading and speaking at evening and midweek services to reduce the responsibility and salary for the interim pastor.

Consider using one of the following two basic interim pastor job descriptions and feel free to edit them to fit your congregation's specific needs and culture.

Interim job description after a hurtful departure:

The interim pastor will focus on helping the people heal from the previous pastor's departure. Through sermons, teachings, and conversations, the interim should help the congregation forgive, grow, and anticipate a positive future direction for the church.

The interim must prepare the way for the eventual first Sunday of the new pastor.

The interim must be attentive to minister to all ages and must help the congregation deal with any sin issues.

The interim is responsible to help the church address any cosmetic issues within the church and parsonage (if applicable).

Interim job description after a healthy, albeit difficult, departure:

> The interim pastor will focus on helping the church keep its momentum and positive anticipation strong. Such duties include preparing and preaching sermons, teaching, counseling, advising, and helping the congregation focus on discipleship, volunteer work, and strong commitment. The interim helps everyone anticipate the positive future direction of the church without plotting the details of that direction, leaving long-term vision casting for the new pastor.
>
> The interim must prepare the way for the eventual first Sunday of the new pastor.
>
> The interim must be attentive to minister to all ages and must help the congregation deal with any sin issues.
>
> The interim is responsible to help the church address any cosmetic issues within the church and parsonage (if applicable).

The congregation may wish to spell out actions that interims should refrain from doing, such as initiating new programs without the collective consent of church leadership, campaigning for any particular pastoral candidate, and making any staff or volunteer changes. While the interim may genuinely provide guidance toward improving the congregation based on the church analysis conducted by the search committee (see chapter 10), that role should be advisory and not autocratic.

Your interim should be paid a fair wage that reflects the interim's level of responsibility, including the preparation that goes into the weekly sermons. Other factors to consider when setting the interim's salary include travel or driving distance and other expenses. Be clear about what will be paid and reimbursed. Interim pay is temporary and, when limited to short periods, will not require benefits like those of full-time employees. Clearly defining various aspects of the expected role of the interim should remove any tension, hard feelings, or resentment. An interim should agree up front not to assume too much or to step over the designated lines of responsibility.

Remember that what may be obvious to everyone involved is not always obvious to the interim unless written guidelines are provided. Make sure you follow the non-negotiable rules described elsewhere in this handbook. If the interim's roles are unclear, fractures and divisions can occur in your congregation.

We strongly recommend that you use a written agreement with your interim so there is no confusion or question about that role. Legal counsel can help you finalize the terms and include clear dispute resolution procedures if the interim needs to be reined in or dismissed.

Also, remember that the interim role is designed to be temporary and transitional. The interim does not "become the pastor," so duties can be split among various leaders. The chair of the leadership board might assume all oversight of the finances and make business decisions while the interim pastor focuses on preaching and the spiritual health of the church.

If you have other employees in the organization, always make clear to whom they should report during this time of transition. Preferably, other staff members should report to church leadership rather than directly to the interim, to avoid developing any unhealthy dependencies.

8

Planning Guidelines for Selecting an Interim Pastor

Selecting an interim pastor helps maintain the health of the church while the search committee is at work. The church must maintain forward momentum even in the absence of a lead pastor. Think about the needs of newer members or attendees who may second guess their decision to be a part of your congregation during this period of time. Handling the transition with competence will go a long way toward reassuring everyone. It is imperative that the church's donors maintain confidence and keep giving or the church will find itself financially hurting.

The interim should keep up the morale of the congregation after losing the lead pastor. Regardless of the circumstances surrounding the departure, the interim, leadership council or board, and remaining staff (or critical lay leaders) should also begin focusing the congregation on the future. The recent past may be scarring, but the best path to healing includes hope and a positive forward outlook.

When a church finds itself in any crisis (such as losing a pastor or facing a lawsuit), it is critical to understand that people do not come to church wanting to focus on the *church's* problems. Rather, they come to church to find help with their *own* problems. It is crucial therefore to keep a positive attitude during this time of pastoral transition.

Consider the following as non-negotiables when selecting an interim:

1. Avoid selecting an interim who could also become a candidate. Like a couple who breaks up, the rebound person often appears perfect at first. People in the congregation may quickly fall in love with the interim because of the newness or freshness of the approach and other attractive attributes. At this stage, such emotions could lead to a premature and flawed selection. Even though committee members may think they are clear-headed and have a solid idea of what the church needs, give your discernment time to recalibrate.

   Choose a person who will love your congregation and preach messages of healing. Interims, when not positioned to potentially become the new pastor, can more objectively guide the congregation. Only when you remove the interim from the potential status of being a candidate can that interim objectively preach, counsel, and generally guide the congregation through this transition period. You want your interim to be focused on preparing the congregation for its new pastor—not on career advancement.

2. Educate your congregation about the purpose of an interim and why clear guidelines must exist. And then make it known to the congregation that the interim is not going to be considered as a candidate. This type of communication is imperative, so the church members fully understand the terms and conditions of the interim's role.

This guideline is especially important if the interim lead pastor is another member of the church's pastoral staff. Both the interim and the congregation must agree on the front end not to allow an emotional connection or simple convenience to be the deciding factor in choosing the new pastor. Big decisions come with far-reaching consequences.

Furthermore, if the current pastor is retiring or otherwise leaving the church on good terms, the pastor should, nevertheless, be recused from the search process during the interim period (unless the congregation expects the pastor to suggest a successor). While the departing pastor might be the best person to explain to the congregation the reason for the interim and for the organized search process, after performing that role, the pastor should (at least temporarily) step away from the church until the new pastor is found—and perhaps until after the new pastor has been given a reasonable time to cement that new relationship with the church.

Occasionally, making an exception to the above "non-negotiables" might be in the church's best interest. Because the church has previously vetted all of its pastoral staff members, one of them might be tasked to serve as the interim and even be considered as a candidate. That staff member knows the church well and should have no issues counseling accordingly and preaching what is most needed during the transition. The interim position could, in that situation, function as a trial period for considering whether a current staff member should be called to be the lead pastor.

There is, however, a potential big problem with this exception. If the church does *not* ultimately select the staff member to be the lead pastor, resentment could build, not only in that interim personally, but also in other staff members and even in the congregation itself, which could result in a great deal of division or even a split. Whether this exception should be considered for a particular staff member will depend in large part on the temperament of that staff member and a clear understanding of the expectations for serving in this role.

3. Never select an interim from outside the church's denomination or faith community. Even if the potential interim is a friend of a church member (or related to one, which is worse), **do not violate this rule**. Because churches often violate the first rule of allowing interims to become their long-term pastor, this third rule (if ignored) places them in double jeopardy.

   An outsider could acquire too much influence during a very vulnerable time for the congregation. If the interim lacks an understanding of the church's culture, doctrine, and history, guiding the congregation becomes dangerous because interims take on advisory roles. You cannot afford to allow confusing signals during such a critical transition.

   Sometimes a potential interim from outside the church's faith community might offer to agree to the church's doctrine, culture, and beliefs. However, would any person willing to change those beliefs or core doctrinal positions merely to attain a position have sufficient convictions to be worthy of teaching others? The seemingly innocent act of reaching beyond the church's denominational or faith network pulls more churches away from their inherent identity and support system than any other action.

When the interim does not reflect the church's historic faith foundations, the beliefs of the members, and the legal aspects of their church bylaws, the church could quickly (and perhaps even unknowingly) change its basic identity without considering the consequences. Ignoring such a potential identity change is equivalent to Daniel failing to purpose in his heart not to do what was right when presented with a choice of following the Babylonian king or his own Jewish culture and beliefs.

These rules for selecting an interim exist to help buffer the congregation's raw emotions during its vulnerable time without a leader. Educate the church on these three rules, and your transition will be more pleasant, less hurried, and will produce a more objective result.

9

Evaluating Legal and Financial Considerations

If the prior pastor's departure was a healthy one, the church probably doesn't need to concern itself with any significant legal issues surrounding that departure. However, if that departure was hurtful, the church could be dealing with threatened lawsuits, potential criminal charges, or other legal matters—NOT what the church wants to be doing now or anytime in the future. Many of the legal issues that arise with the search and hire of a new pastor can be avoided or at least greatly minimized by addressing important items ahead of time.

Prior to beginning the search process for a new pastor, the church should consider the issues described in this chapter. Addressing these matters in advance of the search will help expedite the search process, clarify expectations for the new pastor, and minimize the risk that the new pastor's tenure and eventual departure will result in further legal issues.

Update the Church Bylaws

Make sure your church's bylaws are up to date. If they have not been updated in the last five years, the leadership board should take the time to make sure the new pastor is being asked to lead a church that has its legal house in order. Pay particular attention to the scope of the pastor's authority (what do we expect our pastor to actually do) and the statement of faith (what do we as a church actually believe). You might be tempted to wait until you have a new pastor in place before addressing these bylaw deficiencies, but that is not recommended. You want your new pastor to be fully apprised of your church's current procedures, policies, and beliefs and to be ready to fully subscribe to and not orchestrate them.

Additionally, if your bylaws require members to vote on the new pastor, find your list of members, review it for accuracy, and make sure you have an updated list for the actual church vote that is anticipated. Decades of history show dead people vote in government elections. We want to avoid that in our church votes.

There are three main legal benefits to well-written bylaws:

- They protect the church against lawsuits from those who would like to harm the church.
- They protect the church during government inquiries (IRS or local taxing authorities).
- They protect the church against internal disputes within the ministry.

Also consider adding the pastoral search process to the church bylaws before beginning the search, if those procedures are not already there. Including these procedures in the church bylaws serves two important functions:

- It provides a roadmap that's already been agreed upon by the church leadership board and the congregation (if the congregation votes on bylaws changes), which will minimize any conflicts that may otherwise arise in the procedural aspects of searching for a new pastor. The church can then use these procedures in the search process for this pastor and for any new pastoral hires in the future (keeping in mind that the bylaws can always be amended to address processes that did or didn't work during the current search).

- It will minimize the likelihood of any one person or group exercising or having undue influence over the choice of a new pastor. These procedures should require that the search committee be comprised, to the extent possible, of a representative cross section of the church. It should also specify how those selections are made (i.e., by the church leadership board, by a congregation vote, or by some combination of the two).

Develop a Draft of the New Pastor's Employment Contract

Although the following list is not exhaustive of what should be in the pastor's employment contract, the matters described below are those that tend to create the biggest legal issues if left unaddressed.

Tax status: Ensure the contract clarifies—and the pastor understands—the dual tax status of pastors. This means that pastors are treated as employees for purposes of federal income taxes and that the church will file a W-2 for the pastor (usually). However, pastors must make sure their income taxes are paid—the church is not required to withhold them—although the church and pastor can agree that the church will withhold those taxes from the pastor's salary to cover any tax liability. This arrangement is unlike most other employment relationships in which the employer is required to withhold federal income taxes from an employee's pay. On the other hand, pastors are treated as independent contractors for purposes of social security and Medicare, which means the church does *not* withhold those taxes or contribute the usual "employer amount" of those taxes for the pastor; the pastor is liable for the entire amount of these

"Self-Employment Contributions" (SECA) taxes and must file these estimated taxes quarterly. This is similar to non-pastoral independent contractors who have to pay their own FICA taxes. If a housing allowance is part of the church's compensation package, no income tax is due on that amount, but the pastor must still pay Medicare and social security taxes on it.

Duties and expectations: These need to be clearly expressed and should include whether this is full-time or part-time employment, how the pastor's performance will be reviewed, etc. Taking the time to be clear up front about these issues can avoid misunderstandings and disagreements in the future.

Compensation package: Few people seek to become a pastor for the money they'll be earning. But pastors must be fairly compensated so they can focus on the ministry and not on looking for other ways to keep food on their table. The board should set the beginning salary and benefits package (and then revisit these amounts annually), making sure, if at all possible, it is at least equivalent to or better than the salary and benefits of other ministry leaders in the same region with approximately the same-sized congregation, education, and experience. Remember that this job, unlike almost any other, requires working every weekend, continually being in "the spotlight," giving up evenings for meetings, working 55–60 hours (or more) a week, being on call for member medical emergencies, and sometimes even shortening vacations when needed.

There are a number of online resources with comparison tools that provide the board with a means to find appropriate compensation levels based on these criteria. Keep in mind that the more generous the compensation package, the more candidates you are likely to attract.

If the church cannot pay a full-time salary, consider structuring a part-time position and allow your pastor to be bi-vocational. Working two jobs opens opportunities in the community, but the church needs to give your pastor extra latitude in such situations.

Most full-time compensation packages for pastors should include salary, health insurance (preferably for the entire family), retirement (and potential retirement matching), paid time off (or separate vacation, sick and personal paid time), and some extra perks where possible. The extras could include a Christmas bonus, life insurance, dental insurance, vision insurance, professional development, book/subscription allowance, car allowance, paid sabbaticals, and educational assistance. The church also should be sure to approve and record an appropriate portion of the pastor's salary as a housing allowance, which will reduce the pastor's federal taxable income.

In addition to items paid for by the church, some other non-salaried benefits can be helpful. Make sure your church supports your pastor through prayer, encouragement, and volunteering. Protect their marriage by providing marriage retreats and if young kids are in the home, giving them date nights (babysitting). Do not expect your pastor's family to be at church every major holiday; they likely also have family who want them to come home for the holidays.

Don't take advantage of your new pastor's family by under-compensating or taking advantage of their good heart. Due to their commitment to the Lord and ministry, they will probably try to "make it work," but ultimately, their spirits, their commitments, and their family suffers. Too many children have grown up hating ministry because they saw their parents taken for granted, mistreated, and undervalued.

Work-for-hire/copyright ownership of work product: Many pastors are also writers or musicians by nature or by training or come to their new church with extensive other talents and gifts outside of preaching that they will develop and use while employed at the church. It's important for the church to consider ahead of time who will own the work product the pastor develops while employed by the church. This could include sermons, books developed from sermons, blog posts/articles, music written for use in worship services, devotional materials, outreach materials, teacher lesson plans, and other works.

The question of who owns these materials once the pastor produces them should be a point of discussion when candidates are being considered, and it is vital that the church address this issue with a new pastor and include the agreed-upon arrangement in the pastor's contract. The contract should also include a statement that all documents, work product, and other information related to ministry business that are not owned by the pastor must be returned prior to the pastor's departure or at the request of the leadership board.

Confidentiality provisions: Much of what a pastor learns in the role as pastor should not be repeated except under specific, limited circumstances. Pastors are shepherds, and a vital part of that role is counseling and listening to the challenges, questions, doubts, struggles, and anxieties faced by those within and even outside the congregation and keeping those matters in confidence. In the pastor's employment contract, the church should be sure to include a provision requiring that confidential information learned in the course of the pastoral tenure (and defining "confidential" to include, among other things, information disclosed and discussed during counseling and board meetings, member lists, financial and accounting data, information about property owned by the ministry, and other data and information related to the church's ministry business) may not be disclosed during or after employment except with the consent of an individual being counseled, as required by law, or otherwise as needed in the usual scope of ministry business.

Non-compete clause: Many churches have been devastated not just to have their pastor leave under hostile circumstances, but to also have had insult added to injury when the pastor either starts a new church or takes over an existing one right down the road—sometimes even taking half the congregation along to the new church. Consider including in the contract a clause that, upon the pastor's future departure, prohibits the pastor from taking a pastoral role at a ministry within a certain distance from the church (e.g., 10 or 20 miles) for a set period of time (e.g., five years) except with consent of the leadership board. Although non-compete clauses are not always legally enforceable, including such a clause (where permitted by law) should, at a minimum, give a departing pastor pause before considering whether to do something like this.

Conflict resolution: Since the Bible prohibits Christians from taking other believers to court, the contract should include a requirement that any disputes of a legal nature that the church and pastor are otherwise unable to resolve (such as a breach of the non-compete clause) must be handled through a biblically based means of alternative dispute resolution.

Conduct Background Checks

Once you have found a serious candidate you are considering voting to hire, conduct a criminal background check and a credit check and check any references. Background checks can be done in most jurisdictions after a conditional offer of employment has been made, so check once they are asked to become the candidate but before they are introduced to the congregation or are actually hired.

As the leader of the church, including its outreach to children, it is imperative that your pastor have a background check indicating it is safe and appropriate for that person to be around children and other vulnerable persons. Further, being able to manage money and resources for the Lord is a critical skill of stewardship and a must-have qualification in a pastor. Finding out the credit score and debt levels of pastoral employees can be tremendously insightful in assessing their pattern and practice in this area. If someone has a pattern of over-spending or bankruptcies, you can fully expect that pattern to continue with the church's resources.

10

Assessing Your Church

Before you can make your pastor profile, you will need to objectively assess your church. The following questions and issues, while certainly not exhaustive, will help provide guidance for undertaking this task. The answers to these questions should then be heavily considered when creating your pastor profile.

For example, if your church is located in an inner city and is heavily invested in ministry opportunities at the local public school, you would not want to bring in a pastor who wants nothing to do with public schools. Or maybe your church is a multi-campus facility with a budget in the tens of millions. Bringing in a pastor who has always lived in a small rural town, population 250 and regular church attendance of 40, may not be the best fit for you.

Consider the following factors/questions about your church:

- Composition of the congregation:
    - Ages: Are most members/attendees older? Or is the church primarily composed of younger families with children?
    - Education: Do most who attend the church have a college education or even more advanced degrees? Or are they primarily high school graduates at most?

- Occupations: Is the church made up of mostly white-collar professionals or blue-collar people working in the trades, farmers, factory workers, etc.? Does your church have a lot of teachers?
- Racial/Ethnic/Cultural makeup: Are most of your members and regular attendees of a particular racial, ethnic, or cultural background, especially one that is steeped in cultural traditions or a particular language? If so, sensitivity to these factors is quite important. For example, if a large urban church with a heavily Hispanic membership is looking for a pastor, the right fit will likely not be someone who can't speak Spanish.

- Physical size of the church and its facilities/land: Is the church landlocked in a town or city? Or located in an area with lots of available land? Does the church have a Christian school or daycare?
- Church budget: Does the church have and meet the budget fairly easily, whether large or small?
- Geographics of the church and surrounding community: Is the church in a rural area or in the center of a small town where everyone knows everyone and tradition is extremely important? Is it located in a sprawling metropolis with dozens of businesses, a school, and hundreds of neighbors within walking distance of the church? Is its culture northern or southern? East or West? There is a big cultural difference between California and Kansas, or New York City and rural South Carolina. Is it located near a large military base or in the middle of a vacation destination?
- Current ministries: Does the church want to continue, downsize, or expand these ministries?

- Desired ministries: What ministry areas would the church like to expand into if it had the leadership and volunteers necessary to do so?
- Leadership: How formal and accountable is the leadership structure of the church? Do you have one or two families that make most of the decisions and essentially "run" the church? Do you have a number of lay elders and/or other professional staff that help keep the leadership in check? Is most of the work done by the pastoral staff or by member volunteers? What percentage of your members are engaged in some sort of volunteer work for the church? What percentage merely occupy the pews on Sundays?
- Bylaws: Do you have your bylaws in order? Have they been updated within the last five years to reflect the current cultural and political challenges facing Bible-believing churches? If not, it would be a good idea to take care of that before beginning the search for a candidate.
- The needs of the immediate community: Is the church located in a lower-income neighborhood or in a crime-ridden area where poverty or homelessness might be rampant? Is it located in a university town where a lot of academic minds and college-age students live? Are most people in the immediate area already affiliated with a church? Or is there a wide opportunity for reaching the lost?
- History: What is your church's history? Is the church decades old or older and wanting to maintain its traditions? Or is it newer or revitalized, and seeking to implement new methods of outreach or worship?

- Affiliations: Is the church denominationally affiliated? If so, the denomination may dictate some of the candidate requirements or provide valuable assistance in selecting candidates.
- Life cycle: Where is the church in its life cycle? Is it a start-up? Is it growing? Has it plateaued? Is it in decline? If the church is in decline, you may want to bring in someone who has a reputation for turning churches around and getting them on the right path, even knowing they may not stay long term.
- Bible version: Is your church concerned about which Bible version(s) are used? If so, you want this to be clear during the early stages of your search.
- Your community: Is your surrounding community a growing one? Or is it dying with few job opportunities? Are your young people moving away for better opportunities elsewhere? Or are other young people moving into your area because opportunities there are expanding? How many other churches are located nearby? What about medical care? Is there a good hospital nearby? What about schools? Do most students attend public schools? Or is there a large homeschool contingent? Are Christian or other private schools available and popular?

You will think of other ways to assess your church. Potential pastors will want to know as much as possible about your church, and you desire to know the same about them. Write a church description that provides honest analysis (high and low points) and give to each of your top candidates. Churches will often identify areas in which they can improve while doing such an assessment. You can find a church assessement form at FindPastor.com.

11

Repairing a Bad Reputation

Life is too short to never eat the foods we love at the places we love. This is why when we go out to eat, we often check online restaurant reviews. Apps and Google searches provide a wealth of information, including customer ratings, comments, menus, allergy accommodations, and even photos, to help us decide where we want to go.

Before the internet (when dinosaurs still roamed the earth and pay phones lined our streets), people may have looked at a restaurant's health department rating, which was supposed to be prominently displayed close to the entrance. Others would ask locals for recommendations or drive around and evaluate how many cars were in certain restaurants' parking lots during peak meal hours. Regardless of the methods employed, restaurants (like any other business) desire good reputations. A bad reputation generally leads to financial failure and the establishment closing down.

Churches, like restaurants, have reputations. Before your congregation becomes a good candidate for a pastor, you might need to do some repair on your reputation. But it is sometimes difficult for churches to objectively self-evaluate. When you walk into someone's home, you might notice the cluttered living areas, the dirty dishes, and the animal hair on the furniture. But the people who live there are so familiar with the condition of their home that they often don't see how their house might appear to others. Conversely, when you walk into a mansion and see rooms full of furniture pieces that cost more than your car, you might be intimidated by the money spent on such extravagance whereas the owner doesn't view it as a big deal. Why? Because humans tend to become accustomed to and even dulled to things that have become familiar.

All churches go through life cycles. The start-up stage is exciting and new. The hope is to survive and thrive, so people take steps of faith with the founding pastor to make the church a reality. The church then begins to grow, which is also exciting as the church leaps ahead in size and influence. Then one day the growth stops and the church plateaus. It's still an impressive size, but growth no longer happens, and attrition starts to become a concern. The church might even begin a season of decline, just hoping to survive without having to sell assets or start over.

Self-awareness can help your church begin the necessary steps toward recovery and protecting its cherished reputation. Just like a struggling restaurant installs new management, renovates, and offers improved entrees on the menu, your church can improve its image and reputation—but it will take determination, thick skin, and honest self-reflection.

Some churches become defensive at this point and adopt a mantra of self-justification and blame shifting. Consider this example: A rural church has gone through a number of pastors over the last 20 years. Certain families seem to have made it their life's mission to "run off" each successive pastor and "protect" the church. Churches that go through pastors like paper towels must recognize that the common denominator may not be their departing leader; it's often the ones who stay. Other members of the church enable such controlling families to wreak havoc on incoming ministers and their families by turning a blind eye to the problem. Because these families founded the church or still contribute most of the funds that make up the budget, others allow their bad behavior.

How can you discover your church's real reputation in the community? Most congregations associate with other churches in groups, usually at a clergy level. Pastors gather, either at denominational or associational meetings (or "just lunch"), for fellowship and collaboration. Even if your church is independent, the pastor probably still regularly meets with other pastors in your community or with long-time pastoral friends or mentors.

When your church is faltering, find a couple pastors from one of these groups not directly connected to your church. Especially if you have a tough time keeping a pastor, ask these pastors, who will hopefully be objective, what others think about your church. Tell them your church is doing a hard self-evaluation. They may be willing to share with you some comments about where your church is at in its life cycle and what type of reputation your church projects. You might be surprised to hear one of the following three reputation types described: (1) the "glory years" church, (2) the "ladder-rung" church, or (3) the "family" church.

The "Glory Years" Church

Some congregations think highly of themselves because of their past—the "glory years" as they call them. These congregations have already passed their plateau and are heading into a decline. A couple of decades prior, their church was strong in the community, but no longer. The glory years church does not understand why well-known or iconic candidates no longer seek to fill their pastoral openings. If your church history reveals that your last couple of pastors left within a few years, it is quite likely that your congregation's reputation is not favorable.

The "Ladder-Rung" Church

The ladder-rung church is an interesting study of identity. This church seems upset because no pastor stays longer than two or three years before electing to step higher up the rungs to a larger or more prestigious congregation.

The ladder-rung church fails to recognize two critical traits of their recent history. First, while it may be a somewhat healthy church with a limited growth capacity, perhaps it has now become merely a training ground for new or rising pastors. Second, perhaps the church has closed its eyes and chosen not to deal with whatever is limiting its capacity and reputation.

If your church fits this description, ask yourself these investigative questions: *Are we content with helping pastors move up the ladder, or do we want the pastor to stay and help us grow?* Does our surrounding community limit us, or are we limiting ourselves?

The "Family" Church

The family church sounds like a wholesome and endearing term. However, when other pastors apply this label, they may not mean that it is "family-friendly." Instead, they may see it as a warning sign posted to scare people away from hazardous conditions. Look at your deacons, leadership council, trustees, or other key lay positions. Are most of them related? Some last names may have changed due to marriage, but does everyone know that you'd better not cross them? Do just one or two families essentially run your church? Do they hold most of the power? Contribute most of the money? If so, you may be a "family" church, but not in an attractive way. Sadly, most of these "family-run churches" will die along with their controlling members.

As previously stated, if your congregation's reputation includes searching for a pastor every couple of years, you can probably not lay all the blame at the feet of the pastors. The common denominator in each case is most likely the make-up of the congregation itself. A church's inability to see the clues left in the wake of departing pastors or staff generally shows up in excuses.

Diagnosing the problem will likely come from someone outside the congregation who can be most objective. Asking those persons for their honest insight and perspective will often be the start to identifying the blind spots and getting the congregation on a growth path again. The church needs the help of leaders who care enough to be honest but who give their evaluation with a mixture of grace and love. Ask them the key questions: Where is our church in its life cycle? What is our church's reputation based on an honest, objective evaluation by those outside our church?

Talking with leaders from your denomination or faith community can provide healthy feedback even when your most recent pastor has served a lengthy and successful tenure. Often, congregations need more preparation for a search than they may think, and they may fail to see potential land mines hidden down the road.

When suggesting someone else to help evaluate the church from an outside perspective, your first reaction might be, "They don't know who we are or what we really need." However, these "outsiders" typically keep a closer eye on what is happening in other churches than you might think. And while you may assume your church's situation is unique, these pastors have probably witnessed the same or similar circumstances either in their own or other congregations with which they are familiar. Denominational leaders, outsiders, or others within your faith community can serve as invaluable advisors without affecting the integrity of your search process or your autonomy.

When asking for help, you may not like what you hear, and of course you can decide what you will do with the information. But don't be defensive or outright dismiss the information; it was brought to your attention for a reason. Keep in mind that good people with good information will usually make good decisions. Your church can regain its good name, reverse a plateau, and start growing again. But it will require honest evaluation and hard work—two things we know from Scripture that God wants to bless. Your church can start building a new reputation today and attract the best pastoral candidate—the kind of person that wants to come and stay. And even better, the kind of person you won't want to see leave.

SECTION 2

BUILDING YOUR PASTOR PROFILE

12

Before Looking at Names, Understand the WHY of the Profile

Before people go Christmas shopping, they generally make a list of what they want to buy for each person. Of course, that list might change somewhat if they see a good sale or notice something else that would be perfect. They hope to find items like the latest electronic gadget for dad, a coffee mug for a co-worker, a newly published book for mom, jewelry for that sister who likes fancy, toys for the children, perhaps that one video game all the kids are talking about. Taking the time to first prepare a list of what you're looking for will help make your efforts more efficient and productive, even if the list might change as you move along.

But most of us don't make a Christmas list or buy items without considering the individual persons we'll be giving those gifts to. The more you understand the person and what they enjoy, what they dislike, their personality, their temperament, and their overall tastes, the more likely you are to discern what they'll really like. If you take time to consider the recipient of the gift prior to making your Christmas list, you are more likely to be successful in giving a gift they'll love.

And the opposite goes as well. If, for example, your dad is extremely risk-averse, you probably wouldn't want to gift him with a sky-diving trip. And if your mom loves coffee but is not a tea drinker, you wouldn't want to give her an expensive tea diffuser.

The same applies to making your pastor profile. Before you can make an effective and relevant pastor profile, you need to understand your church and what your church needs in a pastor. You do this by completing a church assessment, which will be comprised of the details and characteristics about your church that will help determine the kind of candidate who will best match your congregation. Once you have made a solid assessment of your church, you'll want to consider that assessment as you make a list of the qualities and characteristics you want in your new pastor, which will constitute your "pastor profile."

You really should not look at a single name or résumé until you build the pastor profile. You can easily see the problem if a search committee starts out with a preferred résumé or favorite candidate and then builds their list of preferred skills and traits around that one person. Just as you build gifts around the person and not the person around the gifts, **the pastor profile should reflect the needs of the church—not the characteristics of your favorite candidate.**

13

Building Your Pastor Profile

When a law enforcement agency begins to look for a suspect but doesn't know who that person is, they start by compiling a profile. Maybe you have watched on television how this process works. When they have no idea of a criminal's identity, the law enforcement unit creates a profile that provides likely details about the suspect: physical characteristics, background, education, and personality traits. The profile serves as a filter to help them find their suspect.

You don't have to be a behavioral expert to do the same for your pastoral search. This handbook will help you compile the necessary details about your church to help you create a profile of the kind of pastor your church most needs.

The pastor profile will reflect the sum total of all the search committee's work to that point. It clearly defines your target candidate search criteria and paints a picture of the person for which you are looking. This chapter complements the one on assessing your church because the uniqueness of your church will determine the characteristics needed in your pastor. Below you will find introductory considerations for developing the pastor profile—a process that will continue throughout this section of the book.

The pastor profile helps you evaluate biblical criteria, theological expectations, educational experience and expectations, geographical predispositions, ministerial experience, social media expectations, etc. This section will walk you through how to compile the characteristics derived from those expectations to create a model from which to measure or assess your candidates.

Now is a time when prayer will become even more important for the committee. You are now entering into an area where some disagreement is likely to surface. Make sure your committee is regularly praying together and is demonstrating grace among its members. You will need the Lord's help more than ever as you create the pastor profile that will guide the rest of your time together.

Start by creating tables or lists on a clean page with headings such as "Non-Negotiable," "Strong Preference," "Desired," and "Optional" (or other categories that would define your preferred characteristics). Put them in descending order. Begin by listing your non-negotiables. Keep this list as short as possible; otherwise, you are very likely to screen out well-qualified candidates who have experience or a background that might otherwise easily compensate for some perceived non-negotiables. (Download the pastor profile worksheet at FindPastor.com and use it through this entire section of the handbook.)

For example, listing "earned doctorate degree" as a non-negotiable would, probably unnecessarily, screen out a candidate who has a master's degree and is pursuing a doctorate, has been a pastor for 15 years, or has led a mission board. On the other hand, this list should help to create a hard stop for a candidate who fails to meet your true non-negotiables. The candidate's basic theology and beliefs are likely a category that will be on your list of non-negotiables.

Once the non-negotiables are listed at the top of your profile, make a list of "strongly preferred" categories, such as "Educational Requirements," "Ministerial Experience," and other categories that have made your list. Under each of these categories, list the specific desired qualifications in their order of importance. For example, under "Educational Requirements," you might list "bachelor's degree" as your most important qualification. A master's degree or other type of degree or qualification might be second. Using this sort of rank order in the various categories will help you determine which candidate is the better fit when several appear to be close in qualifications.

The pastor profile will serve as a matrix by which you evaluate and compare all your candidates. Your short list for a first interview will be the top three candidates who match most of your profile criteria and who meet all your non-negotiables.

Take your time with this process. It is likely that various opinions will surface regarding which characteristics are most important and how to rank them. Determining the criteria for specific traits may be difficult, but keep at it. When disagreements occur, allow each person to make the case for their idea and then allow discussion from others. From the discussion a consensus will hopefully emerge among the committee.

If the group remains divided even after discussing and praying about a particular issue, set that item aside and revisit it at the next meeting. It is more common to face various opinions on the preferences than on the non-negotiables. The non-negotiables should be more obvious, based on your church's assessment. While the preferences may be more personal, do not allow a hostile division to develop on the committee or in the church. Again, establishing the profile is one place where praying together will be very important.

The pastor profile layout and format will vary based on each church's prescribed order or priorities. You can download the pastor profile worksheet and a sample profile at FindPastor.com. While this sample pastor profile is **not intended for you to use as-is**, it is relatively universal in that it includes the criteria most churches will need to collect for their pastor profile.

We would strongly encourage you to remember one essential rule of the search process: **do not look at any names or résumés until your pastor profile is completed.** The pastor profile will screen out candidates who do not meet the minimum desired-qualification thresholds. By comparing all the candidate questionnaires against your target profile criteria, you remove subjectivity and increase your accuracy for the best fit. The committee will use this profile to save countless hours sorting through prospective candidates who are obvious non-starters for your church. Let the profile disqualify most candidates while allowing others to rise to the top. Spend your valuable time evaluating those candidates who are closest to your target pastor profile.

In other chapters, we will explore the non-negotiables, the biblical criteria, and other characteristics (education levels, geographical location, experience, spouse and children's expectations, etc.) that you may need to add as you continue to clarify, update, and revise the pastor profile. We begin in this chapter with general characteristics and traits you will want in your pastor *because of the kind of congregation you have*. Completing the church assessment will have prepared your committee to choose the characteristics on the list below (and others, as appropriate) that would best align with your congregation and where you want your church to go. Remember to keep your list realistic and not contradictory. For example, a candidate will not likely be both cautious and a risk-taker. Note the areas below that you think will be most compatible with your church:

List of Candidate's Desired Characteristics When Dealing With Your Congregation

Flexible
Team-Oriented
Problem Solver
Leader
Determined
Motivated
Confident
Humble

Emotionally Intelligent
Authentic
Persuasive
Inspiring
Risk-Taker
Cautious
Enterprising
Organizer

- Detail-Oriented
- Big-Picture Person
- Traditional
- Empathetic
- Good Social Skills
- Strong Work Ethic
- Goal-Oriented
- Dependable
- Enthusiastic
- Calm, Even-Keeled
- Gives Credit to Others
- Self-Effacing
- Responsive
- Positive
- Realistic
- Life-Long Learner

List of Pastoral or Ministry Traits

- Loves Christ
- Loves People (Christian and non)
- Love and Knowledge of Scripture
- Approachable Warmth
- Teachable Spirit
- Discernment
- Quick to Offer Grace
- Patient
- Accountable
- Family Oriented
- Ability to Delegate
- True Listener
- Disciple-Maker
- Sharer of the Gospel
- Generous
- Visionary

Later, when interviewing candidates, you can use your customized pastor profile to get a sense of how each interviewed candidate aligns with those desired characteristics. A person who appears to meet all or most of those characteristics will likely fit in well with your congregation.

The old adage is certainly true that if you aim for "nothing," you will hit the target every time. When it comes to selecting a pastor, it is well worth taking the time to think and pray about exactly what you are aiming to find.

14

Unwritten Expectations

Starting at the trailhead, hikers work toward the peak following the map. Maps show the path, peaks, valleys, and streams, but the maps never show the snakes, panthers, alligators, or bears. Churches may write and provide incredible job descriptions for their candidates, but it is easy to overlook the "claws" of the unwritten expectations that can be sharper than a bear protecting her cubs.

Somewhere around month three or just beyond, new pastors often bump into these "claws"; they start breaking "rules" they did not know existed. The affected church member lashes out at the new pastor for failing to heed or recognize a cherished preference. Or other staff members get frustrated when the pastor regularly goes home for lunch but none of the others do. Or any other circumstance where things have always been done a certain way but are now handled differently by the new pastor. Large churches often have staff handbooks or enough people to guide new staff members through the correct hoops, but small churches rarely offer much in the way of written rules, policies, or practices. For these churches, virtually every rule, policy, and preference is unwritten; but even with those who do have written documents, it is often the unwritten "rules" that create the most trouble.

The church's people and staff may have done things the same way for so long that they forget the new pastor might not be familiar with their unwritten rules or procedures. During the search process, a search committee typically only communicates those unwritten rules that were violated by the previous pastor—not all other rules with which they would want the new pastor to comply.

The following "big seven" are the issues that most often catch a new pastor unaware. Most churches are not sufficiently self-aware to clearly identify these unwritten expectations up front. A candidate will ask innocently, "Do you want to reach more young people?" And the committee will answer honestly, "We most certainly do." The candidate then believes there is a mandate to replace the choir and the organ with electric guitars and teen pop styles, leaving much of the church aghast, never imagining the supposed "devil's music" coming into their sanctuary.

It is imperative that both the candidate and the committee be honest and up front about these most-often problematic issues:

- **Music:** This issue has divided and hurt countless churches, all in the name of worshiping the Lord. People passionately argue all sides of this issue. The goal, of course, is true and authentic worship, but there is more argument than agreement about how music can and should be done in a way that brings glory to God. "Blended" can be a buzzword for upsetting everybody, and ignoring the older church members on this issue can blow your church's budget in a big hurry since many of the younger generation have not yet learned to meaningfully donate money.
- **Money:** Who has the authority to decide what to spend, when, and for what, on behalf of the church? A new pastor may come in not realizing that the authority to spend money is not what was portrayed during the search process. Now instead of moving forward,

a credibility crisis has ensued, and the pastor's honesty may even be questioned.

- **Power:** Who can remove and replace Sunday School teachers and other volunteers? Who has authority to repair or even sell the church van? Who can repaint the church? ... and the list goes on. Someone has the authority to decide these things, and it is very important to convey this information clearly to a candidate during the search process.
- **Bible Versions:** Translations are becoming more of a church-by-church decision, but make sure the committee is clear on this issue with your candidates.
- **Dress:** Casual dress is sweeping the business world, but some churches have distinct expectations on these issues. Churches have split over choir robes being retired, pastors preaching without neck ties and jackets, or women wearing pants to church.
- **Political Activity:** A pastor can under- or over-preach on political and social issues, depending on the expectations of the congregation.
- **Education of Children:** Either homeschooling is the only God-given choice, or it is abusive to deny your child the socialization of a private Christian school or the evangelistic opportunities in the local public schools. It is imperative that the new pastor be in sync with the congregation on this issue. Some churches are a mix of all three, but the private school, public school, and homeschool worlds do not blend easily unless everyone supports and values the diversity.

Unwritten rules often cause the most frequent rifts between the church's lay leadership boards and the pastor, or in the case of smaller churches, between some members and the pastor. While it is impossible to address every issue, the committee should try to provide clear guidance to the pastoral candidates on the most-often-violated unwritten rule categories. Each of the following items has been the source of great tension, pastor terminations, and even church splits.

Bible translations

Pastor's social media expectations

Pastor's community responsibilities

Pastor's dress expectations in church

Pastor's dress expectations in the office

Pastor's dress expectations off the clock

Expectations for pastor's spouse

Dress expectations for pastor's spouse

Social media expectations for pastor's spouse

Church responsibility expectations for pastor's spouse

Community responsibilities for pastor's spouse

Worship styles

Music in worship

Music genres for personal listening

Use of church vehicles

Use of church facilities

Use of church equipment

Use of church supplies

Authorized reimbursement

Permission for changes

Setting up new accounts

Conference expenses covered

How many conferences per year

Travel expense allowed

Mileage or gas allowance
Men's and women's roles in the church
Teens' roles in the church
Children's roles in the church
Paid or unpaid time for speaking events
Vacation time allotted
Reasons to interrupt a vacation
Warranted reasons to return early from vacation
Holiday expectations
Holiday rotation for pastor travel (Christmas with family)
Appointing or changing teachers
Deacon board's responsibility and authority
Handling church discipline
Hiring procedures
Hiring family members (nepotism)
Landscaping responsibilities
Church treasurer role/authority
Church treasurer rotation of role
Business meetings – What items require approval
Business meetings – Who moderates
Business meetings – Annually approved items
Business meetings – Frequency
Political views
Political views expressed in the pulpit
Political views expressed in small groups at church
Political signs in pastor's yard
Social justice issues
Social justice issues expressed in the pulpit

Social justice issues in small groups at church
Pastoral continued education
Reimburse educational tuition
Scholarship for educational tuition
Educational degrees that qualify for assistance
Pastor's kids' grade school choices
Pastor's kids' college choices
Pastor's kids' behavior at and away from church
Pastoral expectations beyond services
Pastor's view on alcohol, CBD, and tobacco
Pastor's view on firearms
Sacred cows—"We've always done it this way" items

15

Determining the Non-Negotiables

If you grocery shop without a list or don't follow the list you made, there is no limit to what could end up in your cart. Meals for the coming week could be challenging because your immediate cravings mistakenly led you to think that Nutella, Greek yogurt, hotdogs, and Coke Zero would get you through this week's meal planning.

In the mad dash down the aisles and hurrying to the self-check-out, you forgot about the kid's breakfasts, the meal for your friends coming over Thursday evening, and the gluten-free pasta. Only when you've checked off all the essentials (and your budget allows) should you feel free to also bring home that half-gallon of Moose Tracks ice cream you've been craving.

When developing your pastor profile, your non-negotiables are your must-haves. Understanding these categories is akin to the list of basic items you *must* have from the store that week to feed your family. As a search committee, your pastor profile list will include all your must-haves along with the characteristics that might constitute strong preferences but are not absolutes.

A non-negotiable in a potential candidate is a characteristic that, if absent, means the committee will not even consider that person as a candidate. Let's discuss non-negotiables in a different way. You would advise your daughter or son that they should not even consider developing a romantic relationship with a non-Christian. This should be non-negotiable. Your son or daughter might have other strongly preferred items on their list of "wants" in a future spouse (such as looks, family background, education, criminal history, and others), but there should be a few non-negotiables, starting with making sure that person is a Christian.

Once you have your non-negotiable list, the search committee should evaluate it objectively. Pray together first for God's guidance and then talk through each item, making sure each member of the committee is in agreement. If you think the list seems too stringent, re-examine it and ask if it is too idealistic. You may need to limit your absolutes to a short list (maybe 4 to 7 items), noting which traits form the "absolute must" (non-negotiable) category, and putting others into another category, such as "strongly preferred."

Just like our budget determines what items make it into our grocery cart, the size of your church (and its budget) may also determine what your non-negotiables are. The easiest way to narrow your list is by examining who you are as a church and where you desire to go.

Honesty requires you to balance your goals with your capacity. Your budget, geography, demographics, denomination, history, and other factors (those items that now make up your church assessment and description) could either eliminate or elevate a particular candidate. Remember, too, you may not be able to afford what you most desire. Part of the role of this handbook is to prompt you to think through details you may not otherwise consider.

Churches that fail to list, or do list but violate, the non-negotiables will suffer pain down the road, and some churches may never fully recover from such a decision. To give your committee a head start, the following are the most frequently determined non-negotiables or candidate must-haves:

- Do they subscribe whole-heartedly to your church's statement of faith and any denominational distinctives?

- Do they meet the biblical criteria for a pastor?
- Are they willing to promise *not* to change your style of worship? Or at least not until they convince everyone otherwise?
- Will they commit to not coming in and completely revamping your church during their first month? Will they agree not to make immediate precipitous changes, but to prepare and bring the members along cooperatively with any major changes in the future? Or does the church really want a drastic change?
- Do they spend time daily in prayer and the Word?
- Are they able to effectively minister to youth, young families, and older adults?
- Do they have a good history of being able to carefully manage money?
- Do they have a good history of being able to lead and motivate people?

If the answer is "no" to any "non-negotiable," you are finished considering that candidate. That way you do not waste your time and effort or place your church at risk.

Think of non-negotiables as the filters used in online shopping. By checking certain boxes, you increase the quality of results to choose from and remove the clutter. Once your search committee has agreed on the non-negotiables, memorialize them at the top of your pastor profile, and agree that these items will not be discussed, deliberated, or changed throughout the entire process.

16

Biblical Criteria

The Bible is not silent about some of the criteria required for pastors, especially those in lead or senior pastoral roles. Neither a church nor its search committee should ignore the Bible as the foundational book for guiding the church in all areas, including the selection of its pastors who are entrusted with the care and shepherding of God's flock. The Bible provides the church with principles and guidance for all of life. What Scripture says should always trump individual opinions.

This chapter is not intended to interpret passages of Scripture for your church; it is to emphasize the importance of ensuring that your church and search committee agree on the basic qualifications of a pastor.

Break down the components of the New Testament passages that discuss a Christian's character and attitude, as well as their aptitude and gifts for leading others. Additionally, the passages in 1 Timothy 3:1-7 and Titus 1:6-9 provide the foundational scriptural qualifications for pastors and leaders. While the whole of Scripture should inform your ultimate selection of a pastoral leader, read especially these two texts and list those biblical character traits you expect to see in any potential candidates. Realize that every biblical trait is important, not just certain ones.

If your church belongs to a particular denomination, association, or faith community, consult with those leaders to help you understand what basic biblical and other qualifications you should be checking. In some denominational affiliations, newly hired pastors will be required to go before a clergy review board to ratify their credentials. Often such quarterly or semi-annual meetings may not occur until three to six months after hiring, allowing the church to get emotionally attached to a person who may not pass the clergy review. Even independent churches should consult with experienced pastors they trust about a candidate's qualifications to serve their church.

It is always a good idea to obtain a second (and objective) evaluation of a candidate before calling that person to be the pastor of your church. Often, that sort of review by another pastor or board will spot problems the search committee may miss. Without some sort of confirmation or ratification of the candidate's credentials, your church could face problems in the future. For some denominational or associational churches, not obtaining this additional approval could result in your church's loss or suspension of membership or affiliation with that group. Consider inviting either a denominational leader or experienced pastor in your faith tradition to sit in with you during the interview process to help examine the candidate. They can not only ask necessary questions about basic candidate qualifications, but they can also help the search committee spot any problems in theological and biblical areas. You will not regret getting the biblical criteria correct.

17

Theological Expectations

Imagine your family of four is discussing where to go for vacation and what places your family wants to visit. How will the family make its final decision? And then who will be chosen to research things to do in the area, determine a schedule for the trip, and make all the reservations? In other words, who will you select to serve as the family's tour guide?

If the family historian or scientist is tasked with making the final plans, that person might focus primarily on all the museums in the chosen area. If the family diva is given that task, the family may end up at all the major shopping malls and gift shops. Ballparks, every one of them, will likely be primary on the list of the family's sport's fanatic. The family librarian may want to take everyone to a cabin in the woods and bring along a stack of books.

Imagine now that this family selection process will not just determine what your family does on your vacation trip—but what your family does for the next ten years. That certainly changes the dynamic dramatically!

Your search committee is, in one sense, playing the role of the family in this scenario. You are being tasked to select a pastor who could well determine the next ten-plus years of your church's theological direction. Choosing that person wisely is the most important choice your church can make.

While theology is a big word that most church members don't use, it is basic theology (which is defined as the study of God and His relationship to the world) that determines the direction of every church. You probably cannot imagine your church becoming "liberal" or becoming a "right-wing cult," but dramatic drift and change can occur because of what might initially be perceived as minor theological differences. Your church's basic theological positions (whether you call them that or not) will determine how and where your church will journey in the future—and not just for a two-week vacation.

In a day when people have less confidence in churches, search committees may feel inclined not to worry about theology, core beliefs, or even denominational or other faith distinctives. Modern, 21st century people tend to want to avoid attaching specific values or labels to their organizations in order to look contemporary, open-minded, or relational, but even without labels values still matter.

The reality is that every human being has a set of beliefs, whether they can or do articulate them. When a person gets placed into a leadership position, that person's beliefs about God and the world (their theology) will be shared, both intentionally and unintentionally, with those they lead. Leaders influence an organization's culture, and pastors will always influence the culture of their church—for good or ill. Your search committee cannot afford to ignore asking key theological questions without jeopardizing the direction and future identity of your congregation.

Your new pastor will (in fact, should) have strong beliefs, a doctrinal theology, and, hopefully, an unshakeable set of moral values. **Your church will become a theological mongrel if your search committee does not care about the theological direction in which your pastor will take the congregation.** Pastors in graduate school study the major and minor differences in theology, but the people in the pews will generally just tend to trust whoever is in the pulpit every Sunday.

To ensure that your candidate is aligned with your church theologically, the church should have an adopted statement of faith that details its doctrinal views as well as its views on other issues of great importance to the church, such as the sanctity of life, marriage and sexuality, the protection of children, and other matters. The search committee should be assured of the candidate's position on each of the issues in your statement of faith before ever considering the candidate for the pastoral position.

Committees often find it easier to evaluate pastoral candidates based on their communication skills or personality rather than on their theological beliefs. But it is always their basic theology that they will be communicating. Be very careful about who you select to guide the trajectory of your church. Remember that your new pastor will be your church's theological tour guide, and not just for a short vacation, but for years to come. Make sure your tour guide intends to lead your church on a path that aligns with Truth and that your congregation will want to follow.

18

Educational Background

Successful pastors are life-long learners. While some ministers have an extensive educational background, others have not had that opportunity. However, there is no excuse for those entrusted to preach the truth of the Bible to not be continually learning and growing. Online education has opened up many educational opportunities for those who cannot afford tuition or travel to a college or seminary. These days costs for online education are not usually prohibitive, and a pastor can also engage in independent study. Candidates who do not value education may be guilty of being prideful in their ignorance—not an attractive candidate to consider. You want your pastor to be continually growing in the knowledge of Scripture.

It is important to note that the pastor's education may eventually influence the make-up of the congregation. Churches seem to attract people with personalities similar to those they see on the platform each week or interact with in other contexts. Likewise, the pastoral staff should, at a minimum, possess at least the average educational background of the church members. If few people in your church possess doctoral degrees, then expecting a doctorate degree of your potential pastor may not be necessary. This principle provides a natural fit for a pastor by building on and complementing your existing culture.

Remember that the pastor leads and should therefore possess the basic skills capable of handling the congregation's issues at the members' educational level. Through reading the pastor's emails, posts, and other written announcements, members will quickly spotlight a poor education or communication style. If your church members are primarily educators or other professionals, they may be annoyed by hearing grammatical mistakes (such as "Me and my boys played ball") or words that don't exist (such as "irregardless"), or the lack of subject-verb agreement, no matter how normal bad grammer may sound to the pastor.

On the other hand, consider that many of Jesus' disciples were fishermen, perhaps with little formal education. Diversity should be welcome in a well-rounded church. Pastoral candidates with limited or no college experience can effectively lead a church. Obviously, however, seeking a good educational match between the pastor and the church is an important consideration.

Leaders who are voracious readers and consume large quantities of books in the areas of theology, history, leadership, and other genres can be very well-educated without ever setting foot on an organized campus or receiving an advanced degree. Most churches would not hire someone who cannot read but may never think to ask if the candidate *does* read. As Mark Twain famously noted, "The man who does not read good books has no advantage over the one who cannot read."

A good and appropriate question to ask a candidate is, "What are the last five books you've read, and tell us about their content." The answer will provide good insight into the candidate's educational level and spiritual and theological interests.

While education is an important consideration for candidates, there are exceptions. Some incredible pastors have never attended a single college class but have been self-trained to the equivalent of a master's or even doctorate level.

Educational levels can be reflective of rural or urban environments and culture. Be aware of your church and your community's educational culture and then find a candidate who matches or exceeds the congregation in that element.

Once your search committee has determined the educational threshold for a candidate, consider inquiring or advertising at specific colleges or seminaries from which an ideal candidate might have graduated. Every college or seminary has strengths and programs that will provide key insights about the candidate who attended there. One institution might be known for being strong in expository preaching, another in spiritual formation or theology, while still others might emphasize practical church leadership. Graduates of each institution of higher education will likely reflect a particular profile, and it would be wise to know these dispositions before, rather than after, finding your top candidate choice.

Talking to other pastors in your area or to your denominational or faith community leaders may also provide helpful insight into the particular characteristics of graduates from various colleges and seminaries. Your search committee's time will be well-spent if it includes doing your homework and paying attention to a candidate's educational bent (see chapter 28 for more) and how that relates to your people.

Remember that large ministries tend to have educated pastors. If you want your church to grow and succeed, look for those candidates who have proven themselves to be diligent in their educational endeavors.

19

Geographical Predispositions

An American pastor began to speak before an Australian group of Christian leaders as their invited guest. His wife had not been feeling well and had stayed home from the service that evening. He asked the crowd to please pray for his wife as she was "under the weather." The crowd gasped, and some appeared to be completely shocked. In Australia, you see, the colloquial phrase "under the weather" means that someone is drunk on alcohol, not that they aren't feeling well. As you can imagine, rule number one for public speaking still remains: "know your audience."

Outsiders' accents, practices, and traditions stand out in noticeable ways and often appear odd to insiders. Of course, exceptions can apply, and sometimes the outsider can fit in well, but don't assume that will always be the case.

People often find it difficult to leave their geographical region and be effective in another region that is significantly different. It would be just as challenging for a pastor from Alabama to connect with a congregation in Vermont as for a New Englander to successfully pastor in the Texas panhandle. Some can make the leap from Mississippi to Detroit and rural North Carolina to urban California. But not everyone can make that cultural transition and minister well.

What will have the people in Georgia laughing and crying as hysterically funny might have the people in West Virginia just staring back at you. Jury consultants make a living helping trial lawyers know how to connect with the people in the region where the jury is from. There is some similarity between preaching and jury trials. Both the pastor and the trial lawyer are trying to convince a group of people who may not necessarily want to be there to do something they want them to do.

The rule applies that people will generally attract and be attracted to people who are similar to themselves. If your church features great musicians on stage, you will tend to attract talented vocalists and instrumentalists to your church. But if your church in Nashville has hokey music, people will say, "you just ain't tryin'" (slang intended).

What most churches do not recognize is that ministry practices change based on the particular region of the country. How to conduct funerals or to conduct oneself when visiting a member in the hospital could vary dramatically from region to region, so pastors must learn the local customs from funeral directors or other pastors who have been in the region for some time. Such details will only come up in the search committee's interview by asking the candidate about regional practices.

Consider asking the candidate to describe their view regarding the use of alcohol or tobacco, funeral procedures, hospital visits, church social gatherings, showers for expectant moms (who you do them for and how), wedding showers, youth camps, retreats, outreach, school sports, and other noteworthy explorations. Search committees may never consider asking such questions because they assume everyone does these things the same way—the way *they* do them. But that is not a valid assumption. How things are done in your locale, as opposed to the candidates' current locale, while not always different, should be another area for the search committee to consider.

20

Experience

There are three main types of experience search committees should consider: (1) life experience; (2) work experience; and (3) ministry experience. Knowing the needs and goals of your church (from your church assessment) will help you determine the levels of experience your candidate should have in each of these categories.

Life Experience: Every person has unique, defining moments that have helped shape their lives. A pastor who almost died from cancer at age 26 will have a different approach to life and ministry than someone who has never broken a bone. Someone who served in the military will look at life differently than a civilian.

A veteran especially will often have a high level of discipline, determination, and drive to succeed. One of the authors of this book served in the military and admits that that experience brings both positives and negatives. The military mindset expects continuous development and improvement and inspects everything. There remains little tolerance for apathy. You can see why a veteran enjoys dealing with details and competent, motivated people but is not as effective in a church that merely desires contentedness and maintaining the status quo.

Another major life experience for pastors centers around how they came to Christ. A person who was saved out of a drug or alcohol addiction will most likely focus on those outreaches. Someone who was saved at church camp, in Sunday School, or in vacation Bible school may have a special attachment to those ministries. Each pastor will always have a special focus based on the ministry pathway that led them to Christ.

Work Experience: Lazy people do not build businesses or ministries. You can generally see whether someone is a diligent worker by looking at their employment history.

Many successful pastors have worked multiple jobs or gig work to provide for their families and help their ministries. In more rural regions of the U.S., many churches do not have the resources to pay a full-time pastor. Church planters go in knowing they will have to work full-time and still pioneer their church. They look for jobs that connect them to their communities and that afford them opportunities to witness to those around them and invite people to their church. For example, barbers have people coming in all day, talking and giving opinions. That is an excellent option for a pastor with that skill who is also building a church. Real estate, insurance, or automotive sales positions can also provide similar networking opportunities for church planters.

Ministry Experience: The length of tenure in specific roles may also be a consideration. However, short tenures should not always sound an alarm. While most committees look for ministry experience, also pay attention to someone who is not currently in ministry but is showing all the signs of commitment, passion, and aptitude for a specific area of ministry. Often, larger churches find age-specific ministry leaders and assistants from within their own member volunteers. Many gifted schoolteachers have switched from education to ministry, bringing wisdom and talent to the position.

Various ministry types of experiences:

Senior pastor overseeing multiple staff

Senior pastor, youth pastor, children's minister, etc., overseeing a multi-site church

Senior pastor of a church with a Christian school

Senior pastor of a church with a daycare

Pastor or staff member managing significant budgets

Pastor or staff member at a multicultural church

Teaching pastor

Family pastor

Executive pastor

College pastor

Youth pastor

Children's pastor

Worship pastor

Discipleship or spiritual formation pastor

Church planter

Pastor who helped grow previous church(es) numerically

Pastors with a mission emphasis

Pastors assisting the healing of hurt churches or split churches

Pastors who lead building campaigns (capital campaigns and actually building)

Seminary or college professor

Denominational position (what department, board, and role)

Professional experience outside of ministry

Use the above list to think about the distinctions of various ministry and employment experiences. Each of the above brings a different value, perspective, and way of solving problems. Often, churches recognize the benefits of those who bring a different ministry experience into their new role.

Some experience can create contradictory expectations. Younger pastors may have little or no experience, but with on-the-job training, they may get it right most of the time. On the other hand, the sage wisdom of the older pastor with 20+ years of experience may not attract young married couples and parents with little children. Neither choice is inherently incorrect, so each church must adjust its expectations based on the experience of their pastor and then find ways to balance any weaknesses.

Experience brings the wisdom of mistakes made, scenarios witnessed, reflections of history, and much practice. But experience also brings baggage, scars, and typically a less flexible approach to ministering. In contrast, inexperience brings new zeal, optimism, novel approaches, and often high capacity. But inexperienced pastors may also require more patience with the mistakes they're more likely to make.

Family-experience expectations are also important criteria to consider when choosing your pastor. Surprisingly, with regard to pastoring their teenagers, parents often trust young recent college graduates, who likely have no children of their own, to advise their teens during the most challenging development years of adolescence. On the other hand, while some churches desire a young pastor to attract younger families, they can then get frustrated when their pastor is not connecting well with the church's older members.

No one pastor is able to fill every box on the checklist. Acknowledging the strengths and weaknesses and appreciating the individual will set up the new pastor for success rather than failure. Every search committee wrestles with not getting everything they desired in their new pastor. Take heart because experience is typically not a non-negotiable. The best advice for balancing the church's desires with the candidate's experience is to do four things: (1) match as many pastor profile areas as possible, (2) discuss everything extensively, (3) consistently pray, and (4) exercise discernment.

21

Spouse Expectations

Sometimes the candidate's spouse gets lost in the shadows during the search process. In truth, the church is only searching for a pastor, not a couple. But the reality is that the pastor's spouse (or lack of one) will generally have a tremendous influence on how the pastor performs that role. A pastor's spouse is an area where unwritten congregational expectations can cause a great deal of mounting frustration over time if such unwritten expectations exist but are never discussed or clarified.

It is appropriate for the topic of spousal involvement to be dealt with during the interview process. It is also appropriate for the search committee to describe the current role (or lack thereof) of the previous pastor's spouse and to ask the candidate's spouse what role they would typically play in the life of the church or what role they have played in previous churches. While the pastor profile should not *require* anything with regard to involvement of the spouse, it is unrealistic to assume that the spouse's role won't matter.

Is the spouse also a practicing Christian? That may not make a difference to some churches. In fact, in one church, the pastor's wife regularly sunbathed in a bikini on the front lawn of the parsonage most Sunday mornings while her husband was preaching. Would your church be amenable to having that family live in the parsonage? Maybe. Maybe not. These are important considerations.

Does the congregation expect the pastor's spouse to be involved in or even lead specific ministries? Teach in the Sunday School? Help with the youth group? Play an instrument or lead worship music? Are there any unwritten social requirements? What about unwritten counseling requirements, such as assisting with pre-marital or marriage counseling? These are important questions that should not be overlooked during the search process. It is very appropriate to ask the candidate's spouse what role, if any, they would expect to play in the church. It is also appropriate for the candidate to ask what role the spouse might be expected to play. Whichever way the church leans—whether toward more or less spousal involvement in the church—it is reasonable, and important, to be upfront about this area of church and family life.

In one interview, a member of the search committee asked a candidate's wife, "What role would you expect to play in the church?" The wife answered honestly, "I will be working full time as a doctor so I will not be available to the church 24 hours a day as my husband will be. However, what I do in the church, I will do not because I am the pastor's wife, but because that area is something the Lord is calling me to do and something that I enjoy."

Another wife answered that same question in a much different way. "I see myself as a full partner in my husband's ministry. Like Hillary Clinton, who famously said when her husband was a candidate for President of the United States, you will be getting 'two for one.' I generally help my husband with administrative tasks, and I also regularly assist with research for sermons."

The above responses, or anything in between, will be acceptable to one church or another, but it is important to know which response will be most acceptable to your church. And if a search committee member doesn't ask those important questions, it is also appropriate for the candidate to ask, "What have your previous pastors' spouses done in the church?" Or "What does your church expect from the pastor's spouse?" The response to that question could be anything from "nothing" to "Our pastor's spouse has always run the Sunday School program, the youth group, and directed the choir."

While only one person is being hired as the pastor and the church will be paying only one salary, there is no mistaking the reality that the pastor will likely be bringing along a spouse, who will or will not fit in with the church's unwritten expectations. As with all areas of a job description and profile, it is best to acknowledge the expectations, both written and unwritten, up front rather than allow issues to bubble up later, causing unintended consequences. No one goes into a new job expecting to annoy or frustrate anyone else, but a lack of honest communication in this area can easily breed resentment down the road.

22

Kid-Related Issues

Premarital counseling covers those important topics that couples may have failed to discuss before deciding to marry. Like good premarital counseling, the search process should help identify any areas where more information is needed about the candidate's family life and child-rearing philosophy.

Like the unwritten spousal expectations already discussed in this handbook, search committees should also address any child-related areas if the church has such unwritten concerns. Most employers would never dream of telling an employee how to parent, how to discipline, what schools to attend, or which activities are acceptable for their children to participate in. However, your pastor will not be just a mere employee.

Your pastor's basic approach to raising children will come up in sermons, in teaching, in counseling, and in many other areas where the pastor and church members (and especially those with families) interact. Typically, very few committees will ask about child-rearing beliefs during the interview process. Yet the Bible says pastors must manage their households in a biblical manner if they are going to do the same in the church.

Churches must recognize that pastors' kids (and staff kids) should be treated like any other kids in the church and should be given reasonable latitude throughout their developmental years. In fact, it is often very difficult to be raised as a pastor's kid, constantly living under the scrutiny of the entire church. In almost every church, there will be members who regularly make their disappointment or disapproval of the pastor's kids known to the pastor, their friends, and the leadership board. Not every child will turn out perfect, and some children are just harder to raise than others.

Take the true story of a pastor who served a small-town church for nearly 50 years. In fact, that church was the only one in which he ever served. He had five lovely children, fairly close in age. The parsonage and church were located in the center of town, just up the street from the town bank. Church members (and other local citizens) were appalled when they learned that the pastor's second son (then about seven years old) developed a habit of slipping out of his house and standing outside the bank, introducing himself to customers, and asking them for money. No one ever asked the pastor if he and the child's mother had ever tried to stop this rather cheeky behavior. But the members still loved their pastor and his wife, despite the child's embarrassing, entrepreneurial behavior outside the bank. Eventually, the boy grew up and no longer panhandled outside the bank. In fact, he grew into a very nice young man. This pastor and his wife had a wonderful relationship with the church, and the congregation was patient and gracious with the child's antics.

Nevertheless, search committees should explore basic areas of beliefs about family life and child rearing during reference checks early in the process, and certainly during a first interview. But keep the topic general and do not particularly target the pastor's actual family or children.

No pastor wants to feel like the family's behavior is being put under a microscope or that the church will dictate how to raise children in the parsonage. On the other hand, no church wants the parenting philosophy of the pastor to be so different from that of the church as to cause discomfort among the church's families. There are some general areas that can be explored to determine whether such unwritten expectations could become problematic. The questions below are areas where some congregations have found issues with their pastors in the past. Decide which of these topics might be of concern to your church and plan your questions accordingly.

One area to discuss from a philosophy of education perspective is schooling. Does the church expect the pastor's children to attend public or private school? Is homeschooling accepted by your church families? Or is private or Christian school the only expected choice? If so, are there some private or religious schools on an approved or non-approved list?

If the church runs its own Christian school or daycare, would the church expect the pastor's children to attend there? Or could those kids attend another school or daycare?

What about college choices? Is a state school or university acceptable? Or would only a Christian college be acceptable? Remember that church families will often come to mimic the choices of their pastor regarding education. It is common to see many church families begin to homeschool if that's what the pastor does. Or other youth will decide to attend the same college or university that the pastor's children attend.

Is participation allowed in city or county recreational sports, and what if the games interfere with church services? Is it acceptable in the church for youth to play in the public-school band? What about the school chorus? Is cheerleading allowed? School dances?

What are typical methods of discipline acceptable to the congregation? What are acceptable types of music for a teen's listening habits? The list could go on, but it should prompt you to think about those areas of child rearing and family life philosophy that would be important for your church. Not all of them will be. But if certain of these areas really matter in your church, then asking upfront about the pastor's philosophy in this area is better than discovering later that the pastor's philosophy of raising a family is incompatible with your church family.

23

Job Description

Most everyone has played the board game Monopoly. Some of you know the rules inside and out and play to win at all costs. But people can play the game in different ways, each convinced their version is the "right" way. When you discover that your expected way of playing fails to line up with that of your friends, conflict can develop.

Here are some rules (strategies) that Monopoly players may differ on:

- Buying properties before first passing "Go"
- Collecting rent while in jail
- Receiving $400 when landing exactly on "Go"
- "Free Parking" awards you all the taxes, fees, and assessments otherwise paid into the pot in the middle

Are these the same rules by which you've played? If not, you can see how frustrations could arise among even the friendliest of players. Determining the rules before the first roll of the dice gets everyone on the same page, even if some variations are slightly different than you expected. The same strategy applies to hiring a pastor.

Everyone thinks they know what the pastor's job should be. So why write a job description? The reason is because clarified expectations help set the "rules"—the expectations—for the new pastor and will also help limit your applicants to those who meet your minimal criteria. The job description summarizes the characteristics and preferred qualifications you've identified from your pastor profile so that you are more likely to attract high-quality applicants who meet most or all of your stated criteria.

Even if your church has previously developed a good job description for the pastor position, the committee should still update it after developing the pastor profile because the church may have changed its expectations or the pastor's role may have changed. Either way, dust it off, digitize it, and update it to match your church's current situation and needs.

Like establishing guidelines for board game play, you want all the parties to understand the expectations before reaching an agreement to hire the new pastor. No person should ever expect to perform a job without knowing what that job entails. A job description should clearly list an overview of the position, duties and responsibilities, required events, expected hours of availability, qualifications, and any expected affiliation with the community or a denomination.

Sample Pastor Job Description

Job Overview:

________________________ (*church name*) is seeking an experienced pastor who is knowledgeable of and faithful to the Scriptures and has a gift to preach, teach, and equip the church for evangelism, discipleship, and service. The pastor must be a devoted follower of Christ and be living a life that aligns with the church's statement of faith and that demonstrates faith in God, a strong commitment to Christ, the leading of the Spirit, and the authority of the Scripture.

Reports To:

This position reports and is accountable directly to the (*name of church leadership board*).

Duties and Responsibilities:

- Preach weekly worship services that are consistent with the Church's mission and objectives and aligned with its statement of faith
- Teach Sunday School or new member classes as needed
- Lead volunteers or staff
- Visit members, shut-ins, and visitors as needed
- Coordinate ministry activities that reflect the mission of the Church
- Provide status reports to the leadership board about contacts, activities, concerns, and needs (periodicity as set by the leadership board)
- Be available as needed on days off for members' major life events
- Schedule regular church office hours subject to approval by the leadership board
- Provide counseling as needed (pre-marital and otherwise)
- Develop relationships within the community
- Other duties as needed or assigned by the leadership board

Qualifications:

- Maintains a strong personal relationship with the Lord; engages in consistent, regular prayer and Bible study
- Has a strong commitment to the call of serving the Lord as a pastor and teacher

- Has excellent interpersonal skills, both verbal and written
- Has discernment to apply relevant biblical principles to current events
- Is able to clearly convey information and ideas through a variety of media
- Has an earned ministerial degree; applicants without a degree or a degree in another field may be considered with sufficient ministry experience
- Demonstrates a desire for continuous personal and professional growth

Compensation & Benefits:

[Include here the salary range and benefits that are to be included. See the Legal and Financial Considerations chapter in this handbook for more details about what to consider for this section].

If you do not develop and agree on a job description and compensation before announcing the position, unwritten expectations will creep in, causing conflict and disappointment. Establishing clear expectations through a good job description and candidate questionnaire process will prevent anyone from having "to pass Go without collecting $200."

24

Create a Candidate Questionnaire

Résumés provide the committee with what the candidate wants them to have but may not include what the committee needs to know in order to compare and evaluate multiple candidates thoroughly and systematically. Most applicants will look good on paper; after all, a résumé's purpose is to highlight the person's highest achievements and their excellent qualities.

Think of a résumé as a photo of that special family moment. The photo does not show what it took to get the baby to smile or the red cheeks and crying that commenced right afterward. A video tells way more than a photo. **Think of a résumé as a photo, and the entire search process, starting with the questionnaire, as the video.**

It is natural for people to pretend to have their act together better than they really do. Some of the happiest-looking couples on social media end up in divorce court, and some of the people who appear to have nice cars, homes, and yachts end up in bankruptcy or prison. We all want to impress when we invite someone over as our guest, so we clean our homes and serve our best meals and pretend that is how we live all the time!

But it is important to understand that résumés, the online world, and special moments are temporary snapshots that may not present a true picture of a person's life. Part of the search committee's job is to look past the exterior and determine what this person is truly like. Furthermore, many of the qualities that will make up your target pastor profile may not be found on a résumé, such as the candidate's personality traits, characteristics, philosophies, theology, and practices. The search committee must push past the résumé and get to the candidate's day-to-day practices and beliefs.

As detailed already in this handbook, the search committee must first create a pastor profile prior to beginning the search for a candidate. The next document to consider is a form that provides all the relevant details you want all the candidates to have and collects all the initial screening questions for all potential candidates. The search committee should complete the questionnaire before advertising the position or receiving inquiries.

You will likely start to get recommendations and résumés before you are ready for them. Assign one search committee member to receive these items and do not disclose them to anyone until the deadline for submissions is past and all committee members are ready to review them. If someone submits a résumé before knowing there is a questionnaire, let the applicant know an official questionnaire will be forthcoming that the applicant will need to complete to be considered as a candidate. Your committee cannot properly do its job without uniform candidate questionnaire procedures. The questionnaire, which provides details about your church and collects details matching your church's target pastor profile, will also inform the candidates about what type of person you're looking for. This sort of detailed preparation by the search committee will pay real dividends at the end.

Eye doctors don't take the subjective word of patients about how well the patient can see; they will use an eye chart and other specialized equipment to objectively evaluate their patient's vision. The questionnaire serves much the same function, with the results telling an objective story and providing quantifiable, measurable answers that can easily be compared to those of other candidates. Such an initial approach reduces the risk of choosing candidates based on superficial appearances, subjective opinions, emotions, or the strongest voices. Every candidate, without exception, should be required to fill out the same questionnaire and provide the same information.

The questionnaire must go well beyond cursory data, such as name, address, and phone number. From it you should gain invaluable insight into the applicant's background, education, experience, spiritual life/qualifications, worship styles, translation choices, discipleship philosophy, leadership styles, and more. The questionnaire can also ask specific questions about the candidate's spouse. It is important that this form have open-ended questions as opposed to "yes" and "no" options. You can ask, "Are you a Christian?" and an applicant can easily write the word "yes" and move on. Instead, you would want to ask, "Please share your testimony and how you came to know Christ." The open-ended model will provide you with far more information than checking boxes.

Avoid inquiries into race, ethnicity, age, or disability. Even though churches may be more protected in these areas than secular businesses, asking these questions creates unnecessary legal risk and could potentially cause a superbly qualified candidate to withdraw from considering the position. Use discernment when trying to seek out information in the questions you ask.

Make sure your committee focuses on performance and questions about the job—not on a person's appearances. For example, in the employer/employee context, telling employees they are "beautiful" could be perceived as sexual harassment. Telling those same employees that they answer the phone professionally would not be legally actionable.

Questions such as, "Do you think you could connect with our community?" or, "Do you believe you are able to work the hours necessary to grow the church?" are performance inquiries and are completely acceptable.

If an applicant will not take time to complete your questionnaire or provide thorough answers, this disregard tells you all you need to know about their lack of compliance with your processes and expectations. If you are not aligned at this early stage, it is unlikely to get any better if this person were actually hired.

You can create your own questionnaire or download the comprehensive candidate questionnaire at FindPastor.com. Once your committee has determined the wording of these documents, have them formatted and designed attractively, turning them into PDFs for easy sharing. A PDF locks in the information, the font, layout, spacing, and any logos or art on the pages. Sending raw word processing or design files can create chaos, which will not reflect well on your church or on the committee.

SECTION 3

Finding and Narrowing to Your Top 3 to 5 Candidates

25

Headhunter Approach

College sports teams actively recruit the best high school players they can find. So do large companies. Such recruitment, however, does not mean that other students or prospective employees should not apply. Knowing when to fill a position with an applicant versus a recruit depends on one major consideration: Who best meets the qualifications and possesses the greatest potential to fill the vacant position? That could be either the recruit or the applicant. Don't limit your committee to one approach.

Sometimes an applicant proves to be a solid, high-quality option—exactly what the sports team or employer is looking for. Other times, it may be necessary to actively recruit a candidate who fits your qualifications. Both approaches have merit and potential. There is no one right way to find the person you need.

The headhunter approach is often a very effective one for a pastoral search. This approach says, "I am actively looking for the best candidate even if that pastor is not looking for a change." You can take this approach with an open mind while also still reviewing those who submitted a questionnaire. Combining the two approaches will broaden your potential candidate pool. Be on guard, however, when you find an applicant who has changed positions every couple of years and appears to always be looking for greener pastures.

Frequently, the most talented candidates will not apply because they are not looking and are happy where they are. However, just because pastors have not expressed interest in your church does not mean they would not pray and give the possibility some consideration if asked.

Sometimes you will find a higher-quality candidate among pastors and staff who are not looking for a change. The headhunter approach suggests that you are actively looking for the best match for your pastor profile, not just passively waiting to see who will apply.

If a pastor is actively looking for a church, there is generally a reason. It is a good idea to find out what that reason is before determining if this candidate would be a good fit for your church. Do not assume that the fault always lies with the applicant. There can be many reasons a pastor would be looking for a new church—and not all of them are unhealthy.

Some careful research can determine the factors prompting a particular pastor to seek a new position. It would certainly be unfair to attach suspicion to every candidate who applies. Some of the best candidates can be pastors or staff of other ministries who need a change, perhaps because they worked under a toxic board, controlling leaders, or with a congregation that resolutely fights change or growth. Or applicants may just be seeking a geographical change, perhaps for better weather, the cost of living, a more favorable political climate, or to be closer to extended family.

With regard to the headhunter approach, how do you find and recruit someone who is not looking? This approach relies heavily on relational connections or perhaps even hiring a headhunter who actively recruits persons for certain positions. Contact the leader of your state or district denomination or faith community. Talk with respected retired pastors, who generally have a wide circle of younger friends. Find outside leaders who know your church well and can possibly suggest potential candidates who will fit your target pastor profile.

Solid pastors who are contemplating a potential change will often confide in their denominational leadership, friends, or mentors, and ask them to serve as scouts on the lookout for a great fit for them. A name might surface that you would not have thought of on your own. Contact other ministers, music ministers, and others who regularly travel or speak at a wide variety of churches, and seek input there. Many of these folks may be keenly aware of who will potentially fit your profile. It is a good idea to provide these leaders with your church description, job description, and pastor profile to further refine their recommendations.

Contact those colleges or seminaries who train your faith leaders and ask the professors and staff for recommendations. The academic world provides one of the best places to find a good candidate. Many of these schools even have good placement departments or officers. If the candidate is or was recently a student, you can gain great insights from what they studied and what their instructors thought of them. Instructors know quite a bit about their student's personalities, habits, and academic strengths. It is also very important not to assume that every student about to graduate from a Bible college or seminary is only 22 or 25 years old. Many older students are seeking a career change, graduate programs, or continuing education. Second-career candidates can often provide additional advantages for the church gleaned from their previous career.

In the attempt to broaden your candidate search, however, be cautious about looking beyond your denominational affiliations or faith community. Moving away from your church's doctrinal distinctives can be very dangerous down the road. (See chapter 39 on "Probing Doctrinal Distinctives.") Search committees who fail to heed this warning can divide the church or bring about significant change in the church with unintended negative consequences. Focus on those candidates whose theology and beliefs system matches that of your church.

The wider you cast your net, the greater your chances will be of finding that one big fish you want to land. By reaching out to multiple places and people, the headhunter approach can achieve great results without ignoring those who contact you on their own. Share your questionnaire (which includes the job description) and your pastor profile as widely as you can. The more information you share about the type of person you are looking for, the more likely you will be to find that person.

26

Keep Your Candidate List Short

It's family night! Where are you going to eat? Everyone is making a pitch for their favorite choice. Dad wants Mexican. Mom wants Italian. Your teenage daughter wants to try a new trendy coffee shop, while your son just wants a burger. Everyone's taste buds are eagerly anticipating the meal they suggested. Nothing else will do. Regardless of where the family ultimately decides to eat, three people will not get what they wanted. Throughout the meal, each of those three will be thinking about how perfect the meal they wanted would have been—especially if the server at the place they went is having a bad night.

A similar scenario can play out if the search committee members share their top three candidate list with the entire congregation. Maybe the intent was good, but it will be hard enough to please all the members of the search committee let alone to get a consensus from the entire church.

Start by setting a deadline for any recruitment activities and to receive candidate questionnaire submissions. Make sure that each applicant—those who sought you out and those you sought out—provides the committee with the completed questionnaire so that you can compare and evaluate them fairly. If any applicant fails to submit all the items, immediately contact them and inform them about the missing items if they still want to be considered.

Compare all the applicants to your pastor profile (see chapter 13). Each committee member should score each applicant (perhaps on a scale of one to ten) based on who meets the most items, or the items carrying the most weight, in the pastor profile. However, an applicant who meets most items but fails to meet the non-negotiables should not be considered as a candidate. Then you can objectively rank all the applicants. We have provided a pastor/staff profile comparison sheet to help you score and rank candidates. Once you have your top three or five, start the initial interviews via phone or web-based video conference. You can then rank the results of these interviews.

At that point, decide if you want to (or are able to) visit any of the applicants' current churches for site visit evaluations. At a minimum, at least visit their online churches, listen to their archived sermons, contact references, and take any further actions that will help you to evaluate fairly each of these top three to five potential candidates. Afterward, you will likely be ready to choose the top candidate for a weekend visit and second interview at your church. This first weekend visit gives the candidate's family a chance to see the area while the committee gets some in-person interaction and more follow up in a second interview. If that weekend goes well, you are ready to do the final background and credit checks and introduce that candidate (and only that candidate) to the church.

By bringing in and sharing details about only one candidate, you prevent unrealized expectations by the congregation about other candidates. You do not want the congregation to feel like the three "losing" family members at the family night dinner. While losing their restaurant choice will only hurt for a few hours, if church members get to hear about or meet the top-three candidate list, they might compare the candidate they wanted against the one who was ultimately chosen—for months or even years. By sharing the top three candidates' names with the entire church, your committee may unduly make the comparison a competition where more than the candidates lose. Every mistake the new pastor makes will remind them of what could have been if only their favorite had been chosen. This unhealthy mistake treats this process like a beauty contest where all the candidates are displayed together and compared to each other by the entire church. It is the search committee's job to prayerfully discern and bring forward the *one* consensus candidate chosen by the committee.

If you bring the committee's consensus candidate to the church and the congregation does not affirm that person or the candidate feels the church is not the right fit, then move to the next name on the list. By doing your work ahead of time and having a ranked list of already evaluated top candidates, going to the next name does not mean starting over. Work your list, rank it, and then present one name at a time for approval by the entire congregation.

27

Evaluating Candidates' Capacity and Potential

In Aesop's classic fable of the tortoise and the hare (rabbit), we find a lesson for evaluating your pastoral candidates. You know the story: The apparent frontrunner, the rabbit, neglected his focus, discipline, and determination only to find the slow-moving rookie runner who stayed on track and never gave up (if you can even call the turtle a runner!) had beaten him. If you had not known this story's ending, you would, like all of us, have predicted the rabbit as the most likely winner. But with the hindsight of knowing the ending, do you think the rabbit learned a lesson? A little hindsight can help us understand and evaluate true potential and capacity.

As noted in the "Probing Doctrinal Distinctives" chapter, past performance is the best predictor of future results. Jesus knew this principle when telling the parable of the talents. You remember the story: Three servants received talents; the master gave the first person five talents, the second received two, and the third was provided with just one. Each of the first two servants increased the master's investment, but the third servant merely maintained the status quo.

"Talents" meant currency or a Roman mina, a currency unit that equaled about three months' wages. Even the servant with only one talent was being asked to manage a significant asset for his master. But the other two servants demonstrated how to add value to that investment. The master praised them by saying, "Well done, good and faithful servant. You have been faithful over a little; I will set you over much. Enter into the joy of your master" (Matthew 25:21 ESV).

Comparing Christ's parable to your search for a pastor should encourage you. Whatever size your church is now, you do not have to find someone who previously pastored a same-sized church. Instead, you should find candidates who faithfully managed whatever their previous responsibilities were and who are telling you they can handle even more, with God's help.

Church growth should not be measured strictly in terms of numeric increases. Consider other metrics, such as enlarging the congregation's capacity for missions, increasing giving, serving the community, or ministering to underserved populations. When you see a pastor helping a small church rise to do more than imagined, you are witnessing potential and capacity.

Let's shift your thinking for a moment. You may want someone who is currently pastoring a large ministry. But don't just assume the candidate was responsible for that numeric growth. Ask questions that will help you determine the candidate's actual role in that expansion (if any). Perhaps the large numbers were there before the pastor arrived and the numbers have actually shrunk under the candidate's tenure as pastor. Or maybe a large corporation relocated their headquarters to just down the street from your church, bringing 2,000 new people to the area, many of whom are now attending the church. There could be a myriad of reasons for numeric growth. See if you can discern those reasons but remember that growth is not just determined by the number of members.

The flip side may also be true: A candidate may be coming from a church that split or ran off half of its members in recent years. Don't automatically assume the candidate caused this decline. The issue may have been some sin or unethical behavior from one or more leaders other than the candidate, such as an affair, embezzlement, nepotism, favoritism, gossip, or other unfortunate circumstances. Whether their previous church grew or declined, or whether they came from strong or weak churches, you want to know how your candidates handled their roles and responsibilities.

Let's assume a candidate hits all your non-negotiables but only three out of five of your strongest preferences. Ask yourself, as in Aesop's fable and Christ's parable, does this candidate have the capacity to handle more responsibility? Will their résumé after five years of working in your church look like someone you would want to be your pastor? If yes, then feel comfortable pursuing this candidate. Base this evaluation not on hunches but on their actual experience of handling the talents (minas) they were previously given. You want to determine whether you believe this person can handle *your* congregation, ministries, geographical location, culture, and problems.

What if the candidate has had little previous pastoral or staff experience to measure? Then look at how they have handled other areas in their life from a similar perspective. How did they do in college? What volunteer positions in churches or other organizations have they succeeded in carrying out? Ask them about their secular job experience apart from ministry and draw comparisons from that in evaluating their potential for managing, leading, and stewarding resources.

People's work ethic, relational capacity, and dedication will show up regardless of what they do or where they work or study. You need to unearth their experience in these areas by asking critical questions, such as how they grew in their responsibilities in their previous role, whatever that was. Ask them how they solved problems. Probe their interactions with difficult people in their previous roles. Ask if they managed budgets, people, or resources.

A young man took a job at a major theme park. He was truly excited to have this employment opportunity but became somewhat dejected when he found out that his sole responsibility was to stand

and sell hot pretzels and drinks at an outdoor food stand in the park. He was willing to do it but felt like he might be capable of doing something more important.

The wise manager saw the young man's downturned spirit and said, "Son, you appear down about your job selling pretzels to our guests, but I want you to understand that we will sell between one and two million dollars' worth of pretzels and drinks from your stand in the next twelve months. I am trusting you with a huge business that impacts our bottom line with millions of dollars." Selling millions of dollars of drinks and pretzels and successfully dealing with the general public was a major life training opportunity for him. He went on to become a successful ministry CEO and church board member.

By asking, observing, and discerning, you can determine if your candidate fits the mold of the tortoise or the hare. Your church needs a pastor with the potential and capacity to warrant hearing the Lord say, "Well done, good and faithful servant!"

28

Educational Bents

Other than a person's faith and relationship to God, the primary shaping influences on how that person thinks and acts are likely their family, their experiences, and their education. Exploring these areas of a candidate's history helps search committees better predict possible ways a new pastor will interact with the congregation.

Higher education shapes people's lives in important ways. Intellectually, academically, professionally, socially, and spiritually, these institutions have a tremendous impact. Young adults generally set their life direction during these higher education experiences. Many meet their spouses and develop a social network. Most will settle on a major that will heavily influence their career path for the rest of their lives. It is often during these years that ministry callings and commitments are confirmed in the hearts of students.

The committee should consider the following when searching for a pastor and evaluating various candidates' educational backgrounds:

- Focus on schools you know and like. Most churches have some relationship with colleges and seminaries they know and trust. Consider contacting these institutions to recruit potential candidates and give their graduates and alumni priority in your considerations.
- Recognize that schools can and do change. Harvard and Yale were originally established to train ministers. Duke was established to primarily train Meth-

odist ministers. But we all know these schools have changed their focus and priorities over the last 100+ years.

- Learn more about schools you do not know well if an applicant from one of those schools applies for the pastoral position. Do online research and consult with other pastors and leaders in your church network to find out what they know. You will need to ask more than one person and compare answers. If you have a district, state, or associational leader, they will be able to point you to their most-trusted schools.
- The age and personality of the school matter. Some schools are in start-up mode and focus on the founder and often on a particular local church. If you are uncomfortable with that person or ministry, those graduates should be lower on your priority list. If you are fans of that founder and church, you could move those graduates to a higher priority.
- All accreditations are not the same. Accreditation that only requires self-reporting is very different from accreditation received after having submitted to a rigorous accreditation process that is difficult to achieve and maintain. If applicable, verify that any graduate programs also carry accreditation. Just because the undergraduate program is accredited does not automatically grandfather in the master's or doctoral programs. There are two types of accreditations: national and regional. It may sound backward, but regional accreditation is the highest one can attain. The rigors of academic expectations for regionally accredited schools are markedly more stringent than those for nationally accredited schools.

Understanding the institution where the candidate attended (especially if a more recent graduate) will provide valuable insights into your candidate. Beyond the caliber of the school, other considerations include the school's denominational positions, affiliations, and distinctives; the school's doctrinal and theological teachings; and the caliber of the school and the graduates, including preachers, it produces—each of which is addressed below.

Denominational Influences

Every Christian college, university, or seminary adheres to a denominational or doctrinal affiliation or a theological distinctive. If the school has denominational roots, pay attention to the distinctives described in their catalog or online statements beyond their core theology. Certain institutions may have started out with denominational roots but then moved to become more independent with a broader outreach. Even in such cases, however, they will state (and likely follow) specific theological and doctrinal distinctives.

When examining the school(s) your candidates attended, ask them more questions if you note that they went to a school outside your church's doctrinal positions. When doctrine and theology matter, a person's choice of higher education becomes as significant as a medical student choosing a particular field of medicine. A candidate may explain that cost or location made the decision as to what school was chosen, but the committee needs to understand how and why that decision was made.

Theological Teachings

Items to look for include the school's views on the roles of the Trinity, Scripture, salvation, the person of Jesus, creation, marriage and sexuality, Heaven, and Hell. While every item in the list is important and should be closely examined, look first at the school's view of Scripture. That statement should acknowledge the inspiration, infallibility, and inerrancy of God's Word as God-breathed to the original writers under the direction of the Holy Spirit in producing the original manuscripts.

The tripod of inspiration, infallibility, and inerrancy are your keys; without this foundation, every interpretation of Scripture becomes suspect. Then look at the statement on God in the three persons of Father, Son, and Holy Spirit. While each has unique roles, play close attention to the statement on Jesus, the Son, being born of a virgin, living a sinless life, dying for our sins, and being bodily resurrected. The view of the Holy Spirit will help you identify how the school approaches spiritual gifts.

Finally, recognize that Protestant denominations primarily divide along Calvinistic and Arminian views. While there is more to it, a main difference between Calvinism and Arminianism deals with salvation. A Calvinist believes a sovereign God, who is all-knowing, predestines those who will accept salvation. An Arminian believes in a sovereign God who grants people free will to accept or reject salvation. While you will want to observe the broad choices a candidate had for undergraduate studies, graduate-level studies typically offer fewer choices when pursuing certain degrees, so a candidate may have had to attend a school that is different from their own core theology in this particular area.

Style of Graduates

This category will be more fluid than the others. A school does not easily change its core theology or denomination leanings without approval from its board of trustees. However, the type of graduate produced often resembles the culture set by the university or seminary president.

For example, certain seminaries produce great homiletical preachers, others theological stalwarts, while still others may have a missional, discipleship, or servant-leadership emphasis. This category gives insights into how or what your candidate may naturally think or do. It is important to understand how they have been taught to conduct church ministry.

Caliber of the University or Seminary

This area involves looking into the school's accreditation (see that discussion above) as well as the general excellence of the graduates it produces. Do you know graduates of the school? If so, what do you think of their caliber? Their professionalism? The quality of their preparedness for career and ministry? Their convictions? Seek out the opinions of other church leaders you trust about the school's reputation who can provide you with important information along with "bents" for that school and any red flags to look out for.

Remember, the listing of candidates' education on the résumé will tell you more than where they went to college. Using these and other clues will provide a wealth of insight for your committee.

29

Verify Education and Ordination

Higher education accomplishments reveal a level of discipline, broader awareness, and a commitment to one's field. Search committees can gain valuable insights from what and where their candidates studied, as well as the nature of their ordination status.

It is incumbent upon committees to verify claims made by candidates about their education as well as their ordination. Many outstanding pastors never attended college or seminary as some never had the means or opportunity to do so. While some had limited access in the past, today the multitude of legitimate online educational opportunities make it possible for almost anyone who truly desires a college or graduate-level education to avail themselves of that opportunity. As explained previously, your pastor's education should ideally match or be slightly above the educational average of your membership.

Never take any résumé at face value, including educational degrees and ordination certificates. Embellished or false claims of earned degrees or ordination can destroy the credibility of a church. Search committees that miss such details share the blame. Believe it or not, otherwise nice Christian people can and do lie—or don't tell their entire story. Adding simple steps to verify education and ordination claims will provide confidence in who you select.

Verifying ordination status is as important as verifying educational degrees. Denominational ordinations are most likely solid but should still be verified. Pastors can also be ordained by individual churches or by other groups. However, beware of "ordination mills" that have cropped up online, where an ordination certificate can be purchased with no background checks, assessment, or follow-up of any kind regarding the character, education, or beliefs of the ordinand. Legitimate ordination groups or individual churches should thoroughly evaluate those they ordain and should have a regular follow-up procedure. When problems arise, there should be a process to revoke or suspend ordination status or employ restoration procedures.

One pastor decided to test the ability of anyone with a few dollars to obtain an ordination certificate. He actually applied for and received an ordination certificate for his *dog* from a fly-by-night online group. The dog was one of those black-and-white spotted Dalmatian "firehouse dogs," so he looked quite handsome in the professional head shot photo this pastor later took of the dog wearing a clerical collar with his black-and-white spots! While nothing should surprise us anymore, this true story provides an important warning for search committees.

Given current laws regarding privacy, institutions are not legally permitted to release information about their alumni or ordinands without written permission from the student (your candidate). Only request this information for those candidates who make it to your short list of top prospects. At that stage, also ask the candidate if any of the education degrees claimed are honorary. Do the same to verify the status of the candidates' ordination.

Anyone holding an honorary degree should disclose that information on questionnaires and résumés to prevent confusion or the appearance of unfounded qualifications. Honorary degrees are symbolic gestures or awards bestowed on a person for various reasons without any required educational courses or dissertations. A claim to an honorary degree without complete disclosure should cause committees to dig deeper for other embellished areas in a candidate's résumé and biography. Likewise, ordination credentials can vary in quality. The source of the ordination should be similarly disclosed and verified.

If the candidate listed a professor or mentor as a reference, call or email that person (more on references in the next chapter). Ask about the strengths and weaknesses of the candidate while keeping in mind that your applicants will list only those people they know will give a good report. Follow up by asking if that listed reference can suggest another professional who might have a different perspective. The goal is to gain further insight into the type of student or pastor your candidate was or is. Ordination counsels will keep records, and most professors also keep records of their students or can quickly recall their personality, creativity, and academic capability. Good professors or ordination councils have an interest in seeing their students or ministers succeed.

While talking to the personnel of the educational institution or ordination council, ask them what type of students or ministers they are known for producing. Every college, university, seminary, or ordination group has a unique reputation that can provide your search committee with valuable information about your candidates.

30

References & References of References

Rule #1 in this Chapter: ACTUALLY and ALWAYS check references. Everyone presumes that the references a candidate has listed will provide only positive endorsements since candidates will likely only list those they know will support them, but that is not always the case. A committee received a résumé with recommendations from three nationally known pastors. Interestingly, all of them had spoken at the searching church during the past five years. As the committee chair called these references, they all said they "barely knew" this candidate but that they had been "called and asked if their name could be listed as a reference." Instead of helping this candidate, this attempted manipulation of the reference process raised major concerns on the part of that committee.

Some candidates' previous employers will only provide you with the dates the person was employed and when the person separated from that employment. Generally, however, churches are more willing to discuss their prior pastor or staff member in greater depth. The key question to always ask, even of a reluctant reference, is, "Would you be 100%, absolutely delighted to have this person back at your company or ministry?"

If you receive any hesitation before answering that question, you can inquire as to why. While a non-ministry employer may be reluctant to answer that question, a church may reveal that there were accusations of embezzlement or immorality or dissatisfaction with a preaching style. However reluctant a prior employer or ministry might be to provide details, any information about prior work or ministry experience is important in assessing your candidates.

Churches can set themselves up for problems if they do not openly and honestly explore prior ministry or work experiences. An embezzler at a prior church will most likely steal money from your church. A womanizing alcoholic at a prior church will most likely repeat the same failings at your ministry.

The search committee can approach the candidate's listed references in several ways. First, prepare a list of reference questions that could elicit the sort of information you want to know about the previous secular or ministry experiences of your candidate. Include questions about the character and ministry style of the candidate as well as about particular job descriptions and the length of time your candidate was employed or served with that ministry and in what capacities. Then email that list of questions to the reference in a manner the person can easily respond to. Another way would be for a committee member to personally call the references with the list of prepared questions. This method allows for follow-up conversation if the reference is open to providing additional information. The end goal is to get an accurate picture from those who knew the candidate in various capacities—as colleagues, in educational settings, in a congregation, on committees, and maybe as friends.

Should all search committee members participate in a reference call? If only one member of the committee is telephoning or meeting virtually with a reference, the other committee members must rely on the designated member's notes unless the conversation is recorded. Remember that etiquette (and some state laws) requires informing the other party of a recording. No matter how well the designated committee member summarizes a call or video chat, there is no way to fully capture the nuances, tones, pauses, and overall impression of how the reference answered the questions. The best option, if possible, is for multiple members of the search committee to be on these calls.

Written email questions and replies allow everyone to see the answers with the same degree of evaluation. However, written responses do remove the verbal cues, hesitations, or exuberant endorsement one often listens for when asking tough questions in person or by phone or video.

Whatever method the committee uses to collect reference responses, you must ensure confidentiality to those who provide feedback. When the reference feels confident in your confidentiality, you will get more honest and detailed answers, whether in writing or verbally.

Once you have asked all your questions of a reference (that the reference is willing to answer), ask that person for the names of additional people (secondary references) you might contact who also know your candidate well. While a particular reference may not feel they can give you a full insight into your candidate, they may know someone else who could assist you with important information.

The search committee should not just ask easy or general questions of the references. Checking references resembles the role of investigative reporting. Digging for troubling information is part of that process, but with the hope of finding none. Listed references often provide biased insight in favor of the candidate, but your job is to get as much information as possible from an objective evaluator of that information—hence the need to also investigate secondary references.

The questions you ask could be quantitative (with answers provided on a numeric rating scale) or qualitative (open-ended with narrative answers). Consider using a 1-10 scale for quantitative questions, which allows for a large variance of answers with no middle ground. Christians tend to rank people slightly higher as a matter of courtesy and kindness, so a "six" on a scale of 1-10 is not necessarily a great response; it is probably average at best.

Some quantitative questions could evaluate the reference's opinion about the candidate on the following characteristics: honesty, theological strength, preaching quality, oral and written communication skills, quality of their marriage, parenting skills, ability to manage money, ability to manage people, strategic planning, leadership skill, ethics, social skills, work ethic, dependability, follow through, community reputation, interaction with teens, interaction with children, denominational or wider-faith community involvement, reputation, staff interaction, volunteer interaction, conduct in committee meetings, overall conduct, and public testimony.

Quantitative questions (scales from 1 to 10) provide a higher-level overview of candidates, whereas qualitative questions (open-ended) offer deeper insights where needed and should elicit from the reference information about the candidate's weakest and strongest characteristics. For example, suppose a reference marks a six, on a scale of 1-10 (quantitative), for organizational ability. You may need to follow up with that person for an interview question (qualitative) to learn more about that answer in context.

Qualitative questions might ask the reference to describe ways in which the candidate tackled core issues that matter to your church: evangelism, discipleship, new members, the elderly, teenagers, children, camps, training, family ministry, special needs, worship style, Bible translations, running meetings, expectations of volunteers or staff, any friction areas among people, and problem-solving. Asking such questions of the references provides insights from the recipient's view to the scenario questions asked of the candidate.

One overlooked area that can create friction in the future is determining the candidate's preferred leadership style: autocratic or collaborative. Ask the reference to describe situations in which the candidate may have displayed an autocratic style and in what areas the candidate operated from a collaborative style, involving input from other leaders or experts. Likewise, if the role of the candidate's spouse is important to the church, ask appropriate questions about how the spouse interacted with various groups within the previous congregation.

Remember that you do not know if you do not ask. Because past behaviors of pastors often repeat, asking tough questions up front helps prevent future frustrations. **Preparing and asking in-depth questions may seem like too much work for a search committee, but the consequences of not asking the right questions can be disastrous.** The references you question will respect your church's desire for appropriate diligence and overall excellence.

31

Social Media Review

How many times have professional athletes, politicians, business leaders, and, yes, pastors made the news for some scandalous remark made on their social media? While the search committee cannot predict future comments by the pastor, the past serves as the best indicator of what words, tone, and topics the pastor frequently posts.

The committee should be mindful who it chooses to conduct a review of a candidate's public social media pages and posts. Get a tech-savvy teen or young adult to aid in this process. By doing so, the committee will cut their time in half for this review. Someone tech-experienced will find the accounts (the ones most older adults do not use or know exist) and can help the two or three other committee members assigned to this review to quickly scroll through the content.

Consider limiting your search to the following boundaries:

Does this person have a social media presence?

Does this person maintain a tone that is compatible with your church?

Does this person post items or "like" or "dislike" items that would concern your church?

Does this person appear to spend too much time online?

Does this person balance online time with other pastoral requirements?

While your church only hires the pastor, the entire family reflects on this role. It is wise to repeat this procedure on the entire family's public social media accounts. It is advisable to ask for ALL social media accounts of the entire family as part of your questionnaire submission process. Always ask, "Is this the entire list of social media accounts for every family member living in your home?" If you spot questionable items on any of these accounts that you do not quite know how to interpret, make a screenshot and document the postings for the phone interview should that candidate proceed to that point in the process. **Your church should look for a pastor who exhibits wisdom and discernment and who consistently represents Christ on and offline.**

32

More Than a Sample Sermon

Decades ago, search committees asked candidates to mail them a résumé and a sample sermon tape that they would listen to on an audio cassette player (you may need to Google that and see this antique!). If you purchased a music cassette tape back then, you had to enjoy it the first time you played it because as the tape stretched out, the quality was never the same!

The committee would read through the résumés and listen to the tapes. Few understood that these résumés and sample sermons represented the candidate's *best* work and not the *average* of the candidate's skills. These two tools for judging a candidate did not reveal the essence of what the church would actually get in the long term.

Thankfully, search committees no longer have to operate in the cassette tape (i.e., the "stone tablet" and "dinosaur") era. Most churches now put their pastor's sermons online. By browsing through a candidate's sermons, especially when they are spread out over a couple years, a search committee can learn the typical way a candidate preaches, prays, communicates, and shares Scripture before ever seriously considering that person for the position. Make sure your search committee spends the necessary time in this type of research when considering potential candidates.

What do you do if a candidate's church does not post its sermons online? You should then request the following information from the candidate:

- Any recordings of the candidate's sermons that may be available, even if not online
- A list of the past two years' sermons and sermon series' titles
- A description of how the candidate prepares sermons, including the tools used to exegete Scripture and study
- How many hours a week go into the candidate's typical sermon preparation
- How the candidate determines the next sermon topic or series
- How far out the candidate typically plans sermons or sermon series (describe the process)
- A description of the material the candidate most frequently uses as illustrations, quotes, or support
- If the candidate has ever used other people's sermons or sermon services (describe how and ask if the candidate has ever plagiarized or used any artificial intelligence [AI] to create content)
- A description of the candidate's sermon style as primarily expository, topical, textual, or narrative

One ministry leader noted that many pastors who say they have 20 years of preaching experience might only have two years of experience repeated 10 times. If the latter is true, that pastor may continue to repeat the same repertoire of sermons over and over at your church with little change. If a pastor has only about 100 sermons, you can be sure you'll be searching for a pastor again after two years when those sermons run out. Someone once offered a famous evangelist the opportunity to preach on television each week. The evangelist politely declined because he did not want to run out of sermon material. He had developed 36 sermons that worked well and was all he needed for his outreach ministry.

The committee should evaluate the depth of a message and the handling of the text. Discover if the candidate favors a topical or expository preaching style or one of the others. Asking how candidates build their sermons and arrive at specific themes or texts will reveal much about their Bible engagement. If the candidate preaches on the actual Bible text (as opposed to primarily providing personal or political opinions), you can know that the sermons are more likely to be built on the truth of God's Word.

If a pastor acknowledges using a sermon service or has a team building the messages, ask how they engage with Scripture. If a candidate does not study the Bible deeply, how can they advise, lead, counsel, or model discipleship? Often plagiarism or the use of AI results from pressure, comparison, depression, or laziness. At best, such preaching does not regularly harvest insights from Scripture. At worst, it displays the hypocrisy of portraying something unearned. Rest assured, in today's world, with powerful search engine devices in the hands of every church member, someone will look up a great-sounding phrase, quote, or something that does not sound like words their pastor typically uses and will confront the pastor with what they find.

Studying, preparing, and refining a sermon helps the pastor's own spiritual growth in the same way that teaching a small group or Sunday School class helps Bible teachers grow. Matching the candidate's preaching style and delivery with the expectations of the congregation is also important. Some congregations prefer a strong and loud delivery style. In contrast, a teacher-like style may be delivered with less volume but with no less passion or effectiveness. Some congregations like their pastors to stay behind the pulpit, while others get bored with pastors who remain stationary. While these variations in style may not reflect the entire congregation, make note of them, even though they are preferences and would likely not rise to the level of non-negotiables.

While sermons are essential, preaching is only a part of pastoring. Churches expect candidates to bring more than pulpit skills to the role, but sadly, they often use preaching as the only, or primary, criterion to select their pastors. Pastors must also be good leaders, even when they have no staff. Ministry always involves coordinating volunteers, time management, and the stewardship of resources. Don't call a pastor based only on the quality of the sermons—and then fire them for failing to fulfill other unwritten expectations. While today's search committees no longer need to ask for those old vintage cassette tapes, they still need to dig deep into the multiple other hats the pastor will wear.

33

Observe Candidates in Their Current Church Setting

In premarital counseling, counselors attempt to help the couple discover what the other person is like when under stress, during an argument, or in other less-than-ideal circumstances. Face-to-face meetings also help the counselor to gauge the nature of the couple's relationship style. Challenging or rare circumstances also tend to reveal the true character of a person just as military boot camps are designed to push recruits to the limits of their physical and emotional capabilities.

The Apostle Paul shared with the Corinthians that he was beaten five times, stoned, shipwrecked, hungry and homeless at times, and victimized by criminals and religious folks. Additionally, he carried daily pressure for the churches. Seeing firsthand how people handle the stress of ministry is extremely important.

While valuable, a weekend visit to your church typically will not provide adequate information on the candidate's temperament, conflict resolution skills, leadership style, or reactions under stress. Even the sermon the candidate preaches at your church will likely be the best one your candidate has preached to date.

Because a pastor's departure can often result from unresolved tensions, too much change, or conflicts, the search committee needs to determine how candidates manage similar scenarios. If one or two committee members can show up unannounced as visitors at the candidate's current church, you can see their natural approaches and not their typical best sermon and smiles. You can also observe the nature of their interactions with their current members.

In today's online world, the committee can also watch services, hear sermons, and get the sense of a typical Sunday morning without leaving home. Watching online, however, only gives you a limited perspective of the stage activities and not a "feel" for the congregation as a whole. Nothing substitutes for walking in from the parking area to observe the culture and see how the people engage with each other and with visitors. All such behaviors reflect the cues taught and modeled by the pastor, who is the key vision caster.

You want to be discreet when making a trip to observe, and no one should know why you are there. Consider sending at least two couples so you can divide up and scout various aspects of the church, depending on its size. However, do not walk in or sit together, as that is a dead giveaway this group is a search committee. It might be best to go on different weekends so you can see multiple services.

Go in with a list of items you hope to observe (see list below). Arrive 15-20 minutes before the service starts. When you walk in, admit you are visiting and ask whoever greets you for a quick tour to tell you about the church. Ask what they are best known for, about the pastor, people, and various ministries.

Depending on the size and security levels, you may not get to see the children's ministry up close. Do not sit up front or in the very back. Sit about two-thirds of the way back so you can observe the people and the pastor. Collect any brochures, printed materials, and programs/bulletins, and get more than one copy, if you can do so discreetly. Likewise, take pictures of QR codes to share with others on the search committee. Take a picture of the church sign.

While on-site, try to observe the following:

- What the pastor does before the service begins
- What the people do before the service begins
- If the people are welcoming and engaging
- The details and types of announcements
- The song portion of the service (types of songs)
- The instrumentation involved in worship
- Who and how many people help lead on stage
- The age of the congregation (generations and their involvement)
- How people dress in the congregation and on stage
- The length of the service, and if it started on time
- The furnishings and decor in the sanctuary, entry, hallways, and other areas
- The condition of the bathrooms
- The overall condition of the facilities and if an older ministry, if they've been updated
- If the people seem to love and appreciate their pastor

Remember, not everything seen in and around the church is indicative of the pastor, but it should all have some value for the committee.

34

Evaluate Against Your Pastor Profile Expectations

This handbook has helped guide your search committee through the steps needed to create a target profile that will help you evaluate your candidates. Dedicating a chapter to remind your search committee not to ignore all its hard work by making its choice based on emotions would appear unnecessary. But many churches have done so and have been back to square one far too soon. The pastor's role is not meant to be a revolving door and is one of the many reasons we implore you to use your pastor profile like a road map.

Teachers grade assignments based on answer keys or rubrics. What if your child took an exam but the teacher ignored the answers and issued grades based on which children she liked best instead? A search committee that ignores its profile and only chooses the pastor based on personal preferences would be akin to a teacher doing exactly that.

You did all the hard work necessary to compile the profile, so be sure to use it to measure your candidates, especially those at the top of your candidate list. This can be a long and difficult process. Some of your fellow committee members may begin feeling search fatigue and just want to pick somebody to get it over with or because church members are getting anxious. Even if your church members grumble because it's taking so long, you want to "hang tough" and take the time required to do it right and find the right person. Getting this decision right is far more important than just getting it done.

If you only take one lesson away from this entire handbook, it is this: **NOBODY IS ALWAYS BETTER THAN THE WRONG SOMEBODY!**

SECTION 4

FIRST INTERVIEWS WITH YOUR TOP 3 TO 5 CANDIDATES

35

Initial Interview Process

This chapter will prepare the search committee for initial interviews with the top three to five candidates who made your short list. This interview stage will help the committee determine which candidate should be later invited to a weekend face-to-face visit and second interview at your church.

You should be able to sense, by this point, how close you are to finding the right person. Commend your search committee for using the guidance in this handbook to assess the church and build a pastor profile, and examine the résumés and questionnaires to determine your top three to five matches. At every step, you have prayed for insight, sought counsel from leaders in your denomination or faith community, and you have now completed your ranked short list of candidates.

Your committee should schedule telephone, or, even better, web-based video conference interviews with everyone on your candidate short list. Video conference interviews allow you to see and interact more dynamically with each candidate than can be done with just a phone interview. Up to this point, you have only evaluated your potential pastors on paper. Making the evaluation relational through interviews will now help you add humanity and dimension to the previously submitted facts and descriptions.

There should be one point person reaching out to schedule the candidate interviews—preferably the person the search committee has elected as its chair for the search process. Your church (and the candidates) needs one consistent voice speaking for the search committee.

It's likely that any one of the candidates on your short list would make a great choice, but you need to decide which one you will invite for a more in-depth visit to your church. Plan for each phone/video interview to take from 30 to 60 minutes or more. Include the entire committee in the interview. Remember to allow time for the candidate to also ask questions.

Make sure each committee member has a copy of the candidate's completed questionnaire and the pastor/staff profile comparison chart (remember these and other forms are at FindPastor.com). At the outset of each interview, introduce each committee member on the call and have someone lead in prayer, asking for God's guidance and direction for your church and for this candidate. Then, provide a brief outline of how the interview will go—for your committee's and the candidate's sake—to help keep all of you on task and focused on the job at hand.

You may wish to consider having certain committee members ask specific questions of each candidate so the interviews flow smoothly. Be sure to leave sufficient time for the candidate and the committee members to ask follow-up questions to your planned questions. Ask all the questions on your list, but let the candidate do most of the talking. Also remember to focus most of your questions on the candidate's qualities and beliefs that relate to the job itself; avoid any references to physical appearances, disabilities, or other sensitive areas that might give rise to a legal claim.

Be mindful to note the candidate's body language and nonverbal cues when the candidate is talking as well as when the committee is talking. Is the candidate actually listening? Or is it clear the candidate is already focused on what they're going to say next and is just waiting for the chance to say it? Nonverbal cues will communicate a lot about the candidate.

The questions to ask the candidate could come from three primary places: any information provided on their résumé or questionnaire about which you want or need more details, questions from chapters 36 and 37, questions related specifically to the job description, behavioral questions ("tell me about a time when..."), and any other questions your committee wants to know. The follow-up questions from information provided by the candidates in their résumés and questionnaires will all be different, but try to pose the same types of questions from your committee to each person so that you can fairly compare the candidates' answers to either confirm or re-rank your top three to five list.

Try to group the interviews so you can easily remember each candidate's answers and discuss them. One committee member could be assigned to take written notes during the interviews. If using a web-based video conference, record the interview so your committee could replay answers as needed if someone missed an insight. Compare the candidates' answers when all the interviews are concluded and talk through how each one could best serve your church.

How you previously ranked the top three candidates may have changed, but one candidate should rise to the top after these initial interviews. It may not be the candidate you had initially anticipated, but hopefully the committee will agree on the one candidate who stands out and who you want to invite for the in-person interview at your church.

Once you agree on the reranked order of your top three, reach out to the top candidate to gauge interest in taking the next steps. Remember that during the initial interview, while you were evaluating the candidate, the candidate was also evaluating you. If your top candidate is also interested in taking the next step, immediately thank the other candidates for participating and let them know that while they are not off the list of possibilities, you have decided to take the next step with another candidate. Then start planning the details of the weekend visit/second interview to make it the best possible evaluation for the candidate when the congregation and selected candidate finally meet each other.

36

General Interview Questions

Candidates expect questions during an interview. You have already discovered much about each candidate through their submitted résumé and questionnaire. However, after reading through all the data about them, more questions will arise, needing more information. In addition to what candidates have volunteered, you may still need to ask about other areas. This chapter offers the most common questions asked of candidates who are seeking to serve as a lead pastor and also provides a few other character matters to observe while the candidate is answering the interview questions.

- What goals would you have for our church based on what you know?
- What qualities, skills, or experience do you bring to this position, and how did you learn them?
- Does your family support your calling?
- Does your family support you being the pastor at our church and the possible move?
- Describe your children with regard to their current seasons of life and what you think is next for them.
- Who are your favorite writers, pastors, commentators, and theologians?

- What are the last four books you've read? What did you like or dislike about them?
- What prompted your departure from your previous position(s)?
- On a scale of 1-10 (10 being excellent), how are you with handling details? (explain)
- On a scale of 1-10 (10 being excellent), how are you with managing budgets? (explain)
- On a scale of 1-10 (10 being excellent), how well do you multi-task ? (explain)
- On a scale of 1-10 (10 being excellent), how are you with inspiring volunteers? (explain)
- When dealing with people needing counseling, what criteria determines if you will counsel or refer them?
- How do you deal with stress, and what are the signs of stress for you?
- Describe your calendar system, to-do list system, and how you file essential items.
- Describe your discipleship philosophy and how you see that working in our church over the next three years.
- Describe your outreach philosophy and how you see that working in our church in the next three years.
- Describe what you believe every church should be doing. Describe how and why.
- While in your previous position(s), describe how you led the church through a difficult change and what went well and poorly.

- Describe what the pastor's relationship and position should be regarding the church leadership board and other staff, leaders, or volunteers.
- What is the pastor's role regarding women's ministry and their board or committee?
- What does the Bible teach about women in ministry, and how do you see women using their spiritual gifts in our church?
- Describe two or three mistakes you made in your previous position(s) and what you learned from them.
- Describe the role of the pastor and how you see it interacting with vision, decision-making, and implementation.
- Describe how you mentor or develop leaders around you.
- What are the best and worst purchases you've ever made?
- What is your least favorite part of ministry?
- What is your most rewarding part of ministry?
- How well do you delegate?
- Do you consider yourself a controlling person? What would others say?
- What are your views regarding Bible translations?
- What are your views regarding styles of worship? (adults, teens, and children)
- What are your views about bringing politics up in services or classes?

- How available do you make yourself, and how quickly do you respond to messages?
- How do you respond to disagreements and criticism? (please address both)
- Describe a hiring process for various other positions in the church. Who does what, and who makes the final decisions?
- Describe the termination process for these various positions. Who does what, and who makes the final decisions?
- Describe your quiet time and tell what you are reading and praying about most earnestly at the moment or at sometime within the past year.
- Describe how you prepare your sermons (Refer to chapter 32, "More Than a Sample Sermon," to ask more about this important matter).
- Describe human depravity, the grace of God, salvation, and preservation of one's faith. (Refer to chapter 39, "Probing Doctrinal Distinctives," to ask more about these important matters).
- Describe how one can have the assurance of salvation.

If your church has ordaining counsels or clergy boards at some associational level, they may also be able to provide you with a set of questions unique to your church's affiliation. Ask the candidates to complete their answers to some of these questions in writing and seek help from the ordaining counsel to interpret the candidate's answers. Such writing samples will also help you determine the written communication effectiveness of the candidates.

37

Scenario Interview Questions

Tensions between congregations and pastors often come from misaligned expectations or from how each party handles conflict. Sometimes, judgment gets clouded among Christians when each side believes the other mishandled a problem.

Conflicts escalate when people feel the pastor's decisions affect their lives or positions or that of their relatives or friends. Some former pastors have become unemployed because they crossed the wrong family. But in other cases, the pastor's mishandling of a situation deeply hurt the entire congregation. How do you predict what a pastor will or will not do?

Pastors generally fall into one of the following five categories when it comes to handling problems in the church:

- **Problem Provokers:** These pastors, by their personality, tend to be driven and bossy, like a bull-in-the-China-shop sort-of-way. Oftentimes, they are not self-aware enough to realize what they are doing. They cannot understand why everyone doesn't just do what the pastor told them to do!
- **Problem Obsessers:** These pastors fixate over a problem and allow it to dominate their thinking. They put so much focus on it that they center the entire

church's attention around it. They may even suffer from analysis paralysis—the inability to make a decision because of obsessing about a problem or situation.

- **Problem Procrastinators:** These pastors believe that if you ignore a problem long enough, it might take care of itself. This approach requires minimal effort on the pastor's part but generally produces minimal results or allows small problems to grow.
- **Problem Deniers:** These pastors refuse to acknowledge that a problem even exists. Admitting there is a problem *is* the problem, so if they pretend the problem doesn't exist, then there's no problem to fix.
- **Problem Solvers:** These pastors understand that part of leadership is recognizing the problem, addressing the problem, and pulling in the necessary stakeholders to properly solve the problem.

While no one can predict the future, understanding how a pastor handles the present can provide a good indication of what might happen in the future. Asking scenario questions allows your committee to gain insight into how this candidate might solve a problem and what type of problem solver they might be.

Select from the sample questions below and ask candidates to describe how they would handle the situation.

Scenario Questions:

- How would you go about it if you want to change something within the Sunday worship time?
- A church volunteer is accused of child abuse by a child in the church. What do you do next?

- When hiring for non-pastoral staff positions such as custodial, lawn care, maintenance, remodeling, or contracting, would you tend to hire people in the church or outside of the church? Why?
- Name scenarios where you think a person in a church position should step away from their church ministry responsibilities.
- Should a legitimate reason arise to ask someone to step away from a volunteer position in the church (teacher, nursery worker, musician, usher, etc.), how would you go about doing that?
- What do you do when you have a conflict with a deacon or other church leader and have had more than one conversation with that leader about the same issue but still find yourselves at odds?
- When two deacons or leaders come to you with a disagreement over what is best for the church, what do you do?
- You want to change who handles the finances, writes checks, makes deposits, and keeps records, but the person currently in that role has been there for many years. How do you initiate the process?
- You learn that a teenager of a church family is struggling with LGBTQ+ issues. How do you handle the situation, and do you inform the parents?
- The spouse of a seemingly strong married couple comes to you saying they want out of the marriage. What do you do?
- Someone writes an anonymous critical letter about you to the deacons or other leaders, and copies you

(or not), criticizes you, your work, and maybe your family. What do you do?

- The deacons or leadership counsel come to you with a request for you to change how you are handling something. How do you respond?
- Other community pastors from all theological backgrounds ask you or the church to participate in more significant initiatives within the community. What factors go into your decision-making as to whether or not to participate?
- Other community pastors from all theological backgrounds ask you or the church to participate in demonstrations or protests within the community. What factors influence your decision-making about whether or not to participate?
- The student or youth pastor (or youth volunteer leader) shares an idea about taking the teenagers on a field trip or activity you disapprove of. How do you handle it?
- The student or youth pastor (or youth volunteer leader) announces taking the teenagers on a field trip or activity you disapprove of without having talked to you. How do you handle it?
- You want to improve a policy within the church, such as background checks for members who work with minors, but the congregation does not feel that is necessary. How do you handle it?
- A non-attender or long-time member asks to use the church for a wedding in which the couple is one of the following: two non-Christian partners, one Christian and one non-Christian partner, two same-sex part-

ners, a pregnant bride, or partners currently living together. How do you handle this request?

- What if the former pastor chooses to stay and worship here? What concerns would you have?
- How would you respond if a same-sex couple shows up on Sunday morning for service?
- While speaking during a service or an event, a guest speaker or preacher starts sharing a message or presents theology with which you or your church would disagree. How do you handle it?

While some of these questions deal with "touchy" issues, it is important to ask questions like them during your interviews. Look for biblical, authentic, thoughtful, and practical responses to these questions.

38

The Interview Is a Two-Way Street

President George Washington helped lay the foundation upon which the United States presidency was built. Being aware of how his actions would set a precedent for future cabinets, Washington sought out the best advisors to help him model the executive branch of the new government.

The President went to talk with a man named Robert Morris, one of the brightest financial minds of that day, about taking a position as Secretary of the Treasury. However, Morris declined and asked Washington some pivotal questions, leading Washington to choose, instead, Alexander Hamilton as the first Treasury Secretary. Hamilton had served as Washington's military aide for many years during the Revolutionary War, but the President had overlooked him as a viable candidate for the Treasury post. Only after back-and-forth conversations with Morris did Washington realize he had been pursuing the wrong person to fill this position. Hamilton was a better man for that job, as history has confirmed.

Your search committee will need to ask your list of top candidates many questions to determine which one to bring in for a second interview and weekend at your church. Remember that in all of your diligence to determine who your next pastor will be, the candidates are facing the same challenge to determine if your church should be their next place of ministry. An important part of this mutual exploration is the interview process, which provides clarity for both the candidate and the committee.

Interviews will be conducted with only the top three to five candidates on your list. The interview allows the search committee to find out more than what you have already learned from the questionnaire and résumé. Some of the candidates' answers during the interview will prompt more questions seeking more context, explanation, and details. Plan to spend adequate time for the interviews, getting your answers while also allowing the candidates sufficient time to ask their questions.

The search committee should answer all the candidate's questions openly, honestly, and with genuine emotion about the good, the bad, and the ugly in your congregation. The church assessment your committee prepared as its first task will lay the groundwork to fully answer each candidate's questions. The interview process builds trust as both parties seek honest answers and conduct the interviews with integrity.

While this handbook provides two chapters of sample questions for the committee to ask candidates (see chapters 36 and 37), you can expect that a good candidate will also have questions for the committee.

The following areas present some typical questions the candidate may want the committee to answer:

- The circumstances surrounding the departure of previous pastors or staff members
- Issues of power centers in the church, which could be awkward because most controlling families will likely have maneuvered to place a representative on the committee. If so, allow that person a chance to also respond.

- The most recent significant disagreements between the members and church leaders
- General giving, debt, budgets, and the overall financial picture of the church
- Resources the church provides, such as computers, tablets, cell phones or cell phone stipend, mileage reimbursements, vehicles, parsonage, education assistance, library or subscription allowance, conference expenses, and similar questions
- A copy of the last two years' budgets and minutes of business meetings to get an inside look at what the church values
- The role of leadership boards
- Other ministries connected to the church, such as a daycare, Christian school, food bank, or similar programs, and if such ministries exist, what are the pastor's responsibilities for them

Like you, the candidates will be looking to get as complete a picture as possible of your church so they can also pray about and consider accepting the position, if offered. The more experienced the candidate, the more questions that person will likely have.

Experienced interviewers know that you can learn as much about the candidates by noting what questions they ask as you can from the answers they give to your questions. The candidates' questions will tell you a lot about what each one finds essential, whether they care more about themselves or the predisposition of the church, and how much experience they have had. Listen for all the unspoken clues as the candidates ask their questions of the committee.

Your pastor profile created the ideal for your new pastor. The questionnaires showed you which candidates came the closest to matching that profile. But the interviews bring the committee more insight and clarity into identifying the candidate closest to matching the profile and will identify the top contender with whom you will want to continue the process.

See your interview process through the eyes of President Washington, who initially wanted Robert Morris to serve as the first Treasury Secretary. But when Morris declined and discussed other options back and forth with the President, another candidate surfaced. In the end, Alexander Hamilton, who may not have been Washington's first pick, proved to be the right choice.

39

Probing Doctrinal Distinctives

Should the church sign tell everything about the church or next to nothing? Some churches want to be known by one word such as "Life," "Hope," or "Journey." Others believe that lots of information should be present on the church sign, including denominational affiliations or lack thereof, along with a few other descriptive adjectives that will make it abundantly clear what type of church they are.

Regardless of what the church sign may say, the most influential determining factors of a congregation's beliefs are sermons from the pulpit and discipleship lessons taught in small groups or Sunday School. The content of sermons and lessons will shape the church's theology, values, and culture far more powerfully than what the church sign says.

Suppose your church has faithfully taught curriculum from a denominational publishing house and has selected pastors from and support denominational schools, seminaries, and associational networks. In that case, your church is definitely connected and grounded, perhaps even more than you may realize. Those connections can be helpful when seeking a new pastor. Some important protections and benefits can come with membership in a larger association or denomination of churches.

Even in a day when labels mean less, an independent church, with no official or formal denominational or associational ties, will still have its own distinctive beliefs, culture, and "personality" and will likely, at least informally, associate with other churches, mission groups, or seminaries and schools with similar doctrinal distinctions. These connections can also be very helpful when seeking a new pastor.

The search committee will likely find measuring a candidate's theology and doctrinal positions to be the single hardest task, yet it is the most important. You will want to find a candidate who will keep you heading down the foundational path of your church's core doctrinal distinctives, whether or not they reflect a wider denomination or association.

How can you screen candidates for their theology and doctrine? One good place to begin is your church's bylaws. Generally, churches will include their theological and doctrinal beliefs (also called the statement of faith) in their bylaws or perhaps in another written document. Read that statement of faith together as a search team and make sure everyone understands and is on board with it. The more familiar you are with that statement, the more discerning you will be as you form questions in this area for your candidates. A denomination or association will have a written statement of faith, and its leaders can also be very helpful in guiding your search team with preparing these questions.

Search committees at independent or unassociated churches will need to be even more intentional about discerning the theology and doctrine of candidates. Whether the previous pastor left on good or not-so-good terms, a search committee might be tempted to seek the exact opposite of the previous leader. While there may sometimes be merit in this approach, it should not extend to areas of doctrine and theology. Consider having a retired pastor or missionary or evangelist who shares your church's doctrinal and theological beliefs sit down with your search committee and assist you in preparing questions and alert you to any red flags to watch out for and what to look for in the answers to your questions. They may even sit in as you interview the candidate to help provide insight.

Be careful not to confuse a strategy of ministry with doctrinal beliefs. Doctrine is the essence or core of what one believes, while the strategy of ministry is the programs, activities, and actions of the church. **Doctrine is who you are at your core, while strategy is what you do and how you live out that core. Never confuse the two or settle for only one without the other. Scenario or programmatic questions will be helpful with discerning strategy, but not as much with discerning theology and doctrine.** Working within a particular denomination or other network of associations can help you find the right candidate who shares your core beliefs and will also work with your desired strategies.

Candidates position themselves in the best possible light in interviews and on candidate questionnaires, but beware of a candidate who is trying theologically or otherwise to be whatever you're looking for. A candidate who seems to want to be whatever you want is no different from marrying someone you think you can change. Such spouses and pastors will inevitably default to what they know, especially in tense situations.

In the financial world, investment advisors must always warn you that "past performance does not guarantee future results," yet knowing how the portfolio has historically performed is a good guide to determining how that portfolio will perform in the future. The same is true for pastoral candidates. Knowing their history will tell you a lot about their likely future performance. And researching their past will serve you better than merely listening to their answers in an interview.

In evaluating a candidate's past history, what trends should you examine in order to determine their basic theology and doctrine? The first and best indicator is the type of church the candidate has previously served. If they have served in several types of churches with many different connections and beliefs, they may be loyal to none of them. This should raise concerns about what their core beliefs really are.

Second, examine the candidate's education to determine doctrinal convictions. The type of undergraduate or graduate schools they attended may shed light on their theological and doctrinal beliefs. If you are unaware of the doctrine and theology of a particular school, check their website and the courses they offer. Speaking with a professor from that school might also be helpful.

It will also be helpful to find out where your candidates were ordained. Pastors are generally required to subscribe to the theology and doctrine of the group or church that ordains them. If you are not familiar with the ordaining group, look them up online or seek out a leader in that group to find out more about them. Most denominations or other ordaining bodies have a review board or committee that does ongoing evaluations of the people they ordain. Your candidates will most likely be required to be "in good standing" by this review board in order to maintain their association.

Muslims want to remain true to their beliefs as do Catholics and Jewish synagogues. Some adherents will even go to war to defend their beliefs. Yet sadly, too many churches that have the wonderful truth of the Gospel of Jesus Christ can seem far too willing to let it drift away and follow the most attractive candidate they find, no matter what that person actually believes. It is imperative that churches take the right stand, the right way, and with the right spirit!

Make sure you know what your church believes theologically and doctrinally and that your top candidates share those beliefs. **The old phrase that "if you stand for nothing, you will fall for anything" is certainly true in the world of church doctrine.** Be sure you know what you're looking for in this area.

40

Communication Skills (Verbal, Non-verbal, and Written)

Rule #1 when it comes to public speaking is to know your audience. If you address a judge in court by calling the opposing side derogatory names, it will not go well for your client. However, at a ballgame with your biggest rival, calling the other side names is like red meat to a hungry tiger.

Whether you're watching the online sermons of your top several candidates, or your top candidate has come to preach at your church, you will naturally be evaluating that person's communication skills. When people think of pastoral communication, sermons and teachings most readily come to mind. However, communication involves numerous pathways, including nonverbal traits and clues. When evaluating candidates, consider keeping a simple evaluation sheet covering twelve verbal & nonverbal and six written communication criteria.

Verbal communication appears obvious, but to what do you listen? First and foremost, observe the candidates' vocabulary and grammar. Does it sound similar to that of your congregation? Just as pastors' salaries should represent the average or slightly above what church members make, their vocabulary and grammar should also be at least at or above the congregation's average as well. Pastors should sound similar enough to the congregation so that the parishioners feel comfortable listening to them.

Along with appropriate verbal skills, do the candidates display appropriate gestures when speaking? More than half of all communication is nonverbal. As with conversations, sermons without appropriate eye contact and gestures feel awkward. Developing public speaking and preaching skills takes time, and pastors will each develop their own unique style of communication.

When speaking or teaching, listeners immediately notice passion from the speaker. To inspire or cast a vision, speakers need to exude excitement, depict emotion, and use inflection. Except for Siri or Alexa, monotone computer-like voices will limit the connection and interest level from the listeners. Humor, on the other hand, can be charming and disarming and can break the heaviness of the subject matter. Funny quips work well as long as they are not at someone else's expense.

Each pastor's communication style will find its way into their preaching and teaching. Without question, content does matter more than style. But passion, gestures, and humor will make the content come alive to the listeners. Transferring information verbally provides less than half of how one actually communicates.

Assess other nonverbal communications, such as facial expressions, that also broadcast a message to your congregation. Listening well is essential to effective communication, and nothing signals an air of dismissiveness as much as a person who fails to listen. When evaluating candidates' conversational ability, see if they ask questions and care enough to listen intently to the answers. Great conversations cease to be great when they become one-sided. Along the same lines as listening, empathy shows care and connection between the speaker and listener. Empathy may, in fact, be one of the major prerequisites for ministering to others.

Just as facial expressions and gestures communicate a lot before even saying a word, so does one's appearance. Look at the candidates' and their family's social media platforms. Such posts will allow you to observe how they dress in various contexts. During their weekend on site and the second interview, observe how the candidate and spouse dress for each event, whether just around town to see some highlights or when participating in a second interview or other activities. Dress expectations will differ from church to church, but dress should always be appropriate without looking odd or awkward in the context or setting.

Last but not least, written communication matters far more than most realize. The teachers, medical personnel, and other professionals in your church will always, whether consciously or not, edit and scrutinize all written communication pieces. Most lawyers never go to court, but they all deal constantly with written communication and legal briefings. Such professionals cannot turn off their automatic proofreading even if they try. Just instinctively, as a police officer spots a crime, every educator will notice misspelled or incorrect words.

Your pastor or other staff members will send emails, post on social media, create visuals, and write letters, so their written communication skills are very important. You can evaluate written skills by looking at the candidate's résumé, questionnaire, social media sites, blog posts, and email exchanges. Again, your pastor should be at or just above your congregation's grammar, spelling, wordsmith, and educational level. **People want to be proud of their pastor, but they will find that hard to do if their pastor's communication style, delivery, and mistakes draw negative attention to the church.**

Communication Evaluation Sheet

On a scale of 1-6 (with 6 being excellent and 1 being poor)

Verbal/Nonverbal Communication (sermons and conversations)

Word Choice	1	2	3	4	5	6
Grammar	1	2	3	4	5	6
Voice Inflection	1	2	3	4	5	6
Appropriate Gestures	1	2	3	4	5	6
Passion	1	2	3	4	5	6
Humor	1	2	3	4	5	6
Preaching	1	2	3	4	5	6
Teaching	1	2	3	4	5	6
Listening	1	2	3	4	5	6
Empathy	1	2	3	4	5	6
Dress	1	2	3	4	5	6
Overall Verbal Score	1	2	3	4	5	6

Written Communication (correspondence)

Word Choice	1	2	3	4	5	6
Tone	1	2	3	4	5	6
Personal Connection	1	2	3	4	5	6
Grammar	1	2	3	4	5	6
Spelling	1	2	3	4	5	6
Overall Written Score	1	2	3	4	5	6

SECTION 5

TOP CANDIDATE VISIT AND THE VOTE

41

Criminal Background and Credit Checks

You should never buy a used car without first checking the Carfax history of the vehicle. If a particular car has been in multiple accidents or is subject to pending recalls, perhaps this is not the vehicle for you. Similarly, banks will not let you buy a house without a title check.

Without exception, no adult should work in children's ministries without first having sexual offender and criminal background checks. If children are safe anywhere, they should be safe and protected at church. The congregation will expect due diligence with respect to background and credit checks on your pastoral staff prospects.

Search committees do not personally conduct such checks. Numerous services exist to assist churches and employers with this aspect of the search process. Your committee should never apologize for expecting a candidate to agree to such background checks. A candidate who refuses background and credit checks may have something to hide. In fact, some churches have had candidates back out of applying when they learned that such checks will be required. Most candidates will think better of your church for taking such precautions to protect children and youth, just like your church's young parents value these safeguards in your nursery and children's ministries.

Search committees should not pay for such services for all candidates who apply. The background and credit checks should only be done on the top candidate who has been selected, and they should be done after the second interview, just before inviting that candidate to meet the church and preach for the congregation. In some states the law requires that you have a pending offer of employment before you can ask for criminal background or credit checks on prospective employees.

Not all background check services are equal. No one database currently exists for searching out all criminal and sexual predator history, but some are more comprehensive than others. Pay for and use those services that include all pertinent databases for all states, provinces, and categories. Background checks should include the following: social security number trace, national criminal search, national sex offender search, watch lists (no-fly, terrorist, drug trafficking, etc.), residence search for the previous seven years, alias name search, credit reports, drug testing, abuse registries, and others.

Reading such a lengthy list may feel overwhelming or like overkill. A brief look at the offenses for which leaders are dismissed from churches, seminaries, and other organizations, however, can quicky remind you of the importance of these checks. **You can either pay a small price for a thorough background check now or deal with the liability, legal fees, and loss of reputation later on if something surfaces that you failed to discover.**

Similarly, credit checks can provide a host of helpful information regarding an individual's credit score, debt load, and other financial information. If someone is under tremendous financial stress, it is good to know that prior to keeping them on your candidate list.

Find a service that provides all or most of the searches in one combined search. On the FindPastor.com website you can view a list of recommended background check providers and other resources mentioned in this handbook.

42

The Preaching Weekend

At this point, you are very close to finding the right pastor. Because of your committee's hard work, the congregation has found a top-quality candidate and has invited that person to come meet the entire church and preach during one or more services. The candidate will likely have visited the area previously and met with the search committee for a second, in-person interview, but now the final weekend with the entire church is scheduled. What should that weekend look like for the church and the candidate?

Remember that impressions go both ways. The church should try to make a positive impression on the candidate and any family that comes, just as they are trying to be positively received by the congregation.

A few simple checklist items for the church:

- Prepay all travel expenses. Don't leave the candidate's family wondering if this weekend will financially fall on them.
- Select a nice hotel close to the church.
- Put a generous gift basket in the room. Include some "swag" items from the church along with fruit, snacks, candy, and some soft drinks and bottled water.

- Write a personal note from the search committee and put some additional cash in the envelope and place it in the basket for the candidate as an additional generosity to cover any other needs that might arise.
- Plan to provide all meals for the candidate and any family that comes.
- Decide who will host, greet, or pick them up. This needs to be a socially gifted member of the search committee.
- Create a printed agenda with all weekend activities and times to allow the candidate to know what is expected for the weekend (provide this agenda prior to the trip so the candidate knows how to pack).
- Build in some alone time where the candidate and family can think, talk, and pray.

While you may feel knowledgeable about the candidate, the candidate still has much to process. The family must see your city, community, and the church's people. Think of this preaching weekend as a tour for the candidate's family. They will want to see what houses and neighborhoods look like based on the previously proposed salary and what they can afford. You will have shared a potential salary and discussed the benefits prior to this point.

When people anticipate a move, their primary concerns deal with what their lives will look like and how their daily needs will work. Where will they grocery shop? What are the school options? What is the cost of living? Will their spouse find employment if desired? Will their kids make friends? If a family member has special needs, will they be able to find medical specialists in the area?

The candidate, having prayed and walked this path so far, thinks your church will be the next correct move but likely still has questions. Likewise, your church heard your committee's recommendation and knew this great-sounding candidate was coming. But remember that while you and the committee spent hours looking over the résumé, reading the questionnaire, and listening to countless interview questions, the people in your church have not. **Don't assume the congregation's excitement will match that of the search committee.** As you plan a great weekend for the candidate, plan one for your congregation as well.

On the day the church announces its candidate, share what the search committee has discovered and why they are recommending the candidate. Give specifics. Tell the story of discovering the qualifications of the candidate and not just the facts. Share how well the candidate matched your ideal pastor profile. Tell them about the interviews and why the committee is excited about this recommendation. Inform the church about the plans for the candidate's visit to the church and when and how they can meet and interact with the family during that weekend.

Have the candidate plan to preach during your most-attended weekly worship service during this weekend or all services if you have multiple Sunday worship times. This arrangement gives the church congregation an opportunity to see and hear the candidate's preaching style (of which there are many), preaching demeanor, care with the Scripture, sense of humor (or lack!) while preaching, and other aspects of what the candidate would bring to the pulpit as their pastor.

Set up a question-and-answer session during the weekend for those who wish to attend. This might be held later on Sunday, after the candidate has preached. Also allow the church congregation to interact personally with the candidate. This might be immediately after the question-and-answer session or later that evening or even the following day or evening. They need to be able to ask questions, have conversations in a social setting, and interact with the candidate's entire family. Ask any other leadership boards or committees ahead of time if they would like to meet one-on-one with the candidate to discuss specific items, and try to make that happen if they do.

Plan time, if possible, to take the candidate's family on a tour of your town or city. Show them any famous sites, tourist attractions, the local schools (if they have children who will be attending), shopping centers near the church, and other areas of interest to the candidate.

The church should cover all expenses of the candidate's family coming for the weekend. Think through travel to and from, including meals, hotel, and miscellaneous items. **The candidate may equate how responsible the church is on this trip with how well you will care for the family if they say "yes."** Make it a weekend to remember for everyone involved.

43

The Final Vote and Hiring of Your New Pastor

If you are reading this chapter, you have reached the last step in your search process—or at least you hope you will in the future. At this stage, you have assessed your church, compiled the pastor profile, collected the relevant information on the candidates, narrowed the field, selected your top candidate, hosted the candidate at the church for a second interview and then a later preaching weekend, and the church is now preparing to vote.

Assuming the church bylaws call for a congregational vote to call a new pastor, be sure to provide sufficient notice to the congregation of when the vote will take place. "Sufficient" depends on what the bylaws require, but if they don't specify, you should announce the date of the vote during the main worship service and by email to the congregation at least a week prior to the vote.

Some church bylaws call for a vote the same day as the candidate preaches at the church. This is one way to consolidate the process, and it reduces the likelihood that "factions" will form after the "trial sermon" and prior to the vote. However, moving too quickly doesn't give people time to process the sermon, discuss it with their family, get clarity on issues of concern that may have arisen about the candidate in their minds over the weekend, and pray over their vote. Either way the church does it, be sure it follows the process set forth in the bylaws.

On the day of the vote (whether the day of the preaching or a week or two later), plan to hold a business meeting after the weekly worship service. Dismiss non-members from the service so only members are voting (membership-only voting is typical for most churches, but if your bylaws call for a different procedure, use that one) and wait for members to arrive who might be serving in other ministries around the campus.

Remember to pray with the congregation before explaining the process of voting and who will be notified first of the results. Follow your bylaws for casting ballots, which will usually be by anonymous written ballot—ballots have a simple "yes" and "no" on them and members circle their response. After the written ballot vote is taken and collected, the search committee should tally the votes and share results with the pastoral candidate, to ensure acceptance, and the congregation. Whether you inform the candidate or the congregation first, it is vital that the result remains confidential until the candidate's congregation is informed of the outcome to avoid them hearing about it on social media or from other means—including from others in your congregation.

Some church bylaws will require a specified percentage to approve the candidate. That percentage might range from 50% to 90%, but if this number is not already specified in the church's bylaws, the committee should have determined it and announced it to the congregation and to the candidate ahead of time. The candidate will likely also have a number in mind, below which an invitation to serve the church would not be accepted. Some candidates may even require a 95% vote before they will accept a call. Again, these numbers should be known by the search committee, the congregation, and the candidate before this vote takes place.

Assuming the number of positive votes meets the percentage standard in the bylaws or as determined by the committee ahead of time and the candidate still expresses intention to continue, your search committee needs to finalize the details.

Your new pastor will have already received a conditional offer letter from the church describing the hiring details if the church vote was affirmative and the candidate accepted the call to come to the church. It is now time to reduce those terms of the pastor's hire to writing in an Ecclesiastical Employment Agreement (the "Employment Contract" discussed in a previous chapter). An agreement up-front that contains all the necessary financial terms, work expectations, and dispute resolution procedures can avoid unnecessary disputes in the future.

Once the candidate signs the employment contract, your candidate has officially become your pastor. You've been faithful to pray, search, and exercise due diligence during the process, and God has called this person to be your new shepherd. It is now time to extend love and acceptance to your pastor and to treat the pastor's family as you would want your family to be treated.

44

Celebrating the Calling of Your New Pastor

The great preacher Charles Spurgeon once said:

> My brethren, if we are to see the church of God really restored to her pristine glory, we must have back this plain, simple, gospel-preaching. I do believe that the hiding of the cross beneath the veil of fine language and learned dissertation is half the cause of the spiritual destitution of our country. Jesus Christ came into the world to save sinners. He came to seek and to save that which was lost. I would sooner say these few words and then cease my testimony, than utter the most splendid oration that ever streamed from the lips of Demosthenes or of Cicero, but not have declared the gospel of Christ. We must keep to this. This must be the hammer that we bring down upon the anvil of the human heart again, and again, and again. God forbid that we should glory save in the cross of Jesus Christ our Lord! God forbid that we should know anything among men save Jesus Christ and him crucified! (*Verse Expositions of the Bible*)

The church needs spiritual pastoral leaders—leaders who are willing to preach the pure, clear gospel of Jesus Christ and stand for biblical truth regardless of what the courts or our culture may say is "right" or "acceptable." Remember—keep the main thing (faithfulness to God's Word) your highest priority in your search for a pastor. God will honor that.

Samuel Logan Brengle, one of the great leaders of the Salvation Army, challenged church leaders in his day with these words,

> Leadership is not won by promotion but by many prayers and tears. It is attained by confessions of sin and much heart-searching and humbling before God; by self-surrender; a courageous sacrifice of every idol; a bold, deathless, uncompromising, and uncomplaining embracing of the cross; and by an internal, unfaltering looking unto Jesus crucified. (*Soul Winner's Secret*)

The search for your next pastor will require much prayer and has perhaps already been preceded by many tears. We have emphasized the importance of prayer throughout this book because without God's guidance in this most important of matters, this becomes just another job search. Give this search to God from the very beginning and let *Him* lead the way to the right candidate.

As Peter learned directly from Jesus, to see miracles happen, you have to (1) be willing to get out of the boat, and (2) keep your eyes on Jesus. Then and only then can a water-walking miracle occur. If you look at the storm and circumstances around you and quit focusing on Jesus, you will sink like any other person trying to walk on water. It might seem like finding the right pastor for your church will take a miracle. And it will! But keep your eyes on Jesus. Pray. Submit this journey to God, do your due diligence, and He will bring the right candidate to you.

It has been our high honor and distinct privilege to walk this pastoral search journey with you, and we pray God's richest blessings on your church.

APPENDIX—Website Resources

FindPastor.com contains the following for your search process:

Downloadable PDF Forms

- Pastor/Staff Profile (worksheet)
- Pastor/Staff Profile Sample (example worksheet filled out)
- Pastor/Staff Profile Comparison Chart (to help rank candidates)
- Church Assessment
- Communication Evaluation Sheet
- Pastor/Staff Candidate Questionnaire

Links to Resources

- *Myers-Briggs Type Indicator* personality assessment
- *Leading From Your Strengths* Christian personality assessment
- Criminal Background Checks
- Credit Reports: No link for credit check is provided as we recommend search committees request candidates provide a copy of their credit report.

Available for Purchase on FindPastor.com

- Books in a Bundle Discount (for each search committee member or member of your church)
- Preprinted Bundle of All PDF Forms (multiples of PDFs based on average use – photocopy permission granted)
- Consultation time to meet with your committee via web-based video call from one or both authors

ABOUT THE AUTHORS

Ron Hunter Jr., Ph.D.

After pastoring for 11 years, in 2002, Dr. Hunter began his role as the executive director and CEO of Randall House and D6 Family Ministry, the publisher of D6 curriculum, and cofounder and director of the D6 Conference. He speaks internationally and consults for ministry and business organizations. In addition to serving in the military, he earned his MPA from the University of Colorado and his Ph.D. from Dallas Baptist University, where he teaches as an adjunct professor. He is a co-host of the *D6 Podcast*, has written over 80 articles for various magazines, and has published five other books including *Toy Box Leadership*; *The DNA of D6: Building Blocks of Generational Discipleship*; *Youth Ministry in the 21st Century: Five Views*; *Recalibrate: A New Measure for Family Ministry*; and *About You, About Me: Generational Legacy Journal.*

David Gibbs III, J.D.

Attorney David C. Gibbs III is the president and general counsel of the National Center for Life and Liberty, a ministry organization based out of Largo, Florida, that defends life and liberty freedoms nationwide and provides both legal and practical, best-practices counsel to pastors, churches, and nonprofit ministries. He is also a well-known author and speaker on religious liberty issues. Attorney Gibbs graduated from Duke Law School and is a practicing trial attorney, admitted to practice in eight states and the District of Columbia, the United States Supreme Court, and numerous federal circuit and district courts nationwide. His organization can be reached at NCLL.org.